SURVIVING
THE
SILENCE

SURVIVING

THE SILENCE

A Meet-You-at-the-Front-Door
Approach to Surviving Stillbirth
and Miscarriage

Dr. Laurel Davis, Kelvi Place,
and Janelle Robson

Surviving the Silence
A Meet-You-at-the-Front-Door Approach to Surviving Stillbirth and Miscarriage
Dr. Laurel Davis, Kelvi Place, and Janelle Robson

Produced by Spoonbridge Press
Copyediting by Sarah Kolb-Williams
Book design by Brandi Lariscy-Avant
Copyright © 2025 Front Door Press
Ellsworth, Kansas
Illustrations: Dandelion courtesy of FreePik

First U.S. Edition, 2025

Print ISBN: 979-8-9932199-0-5
Ebook ISBN: 979-8-9932199-1-2
Library of Congress Control Number: 2025920527

Printed in the U.S.A.

In memory and honor of Forrest, Eli, and Karaline

Dedicated to the women who find themselves grieving the loss of a little one. To the women who find themselves on the path of loss and love, joy and grief, hurt and healing. To all the women who have suffered a silent loss through miscarriage, stillbirth, or infant loss: This is for you as you journey forward.

Contents

Foreword

As an obstetrician, I find myself in awe of the miracle of life every day. How incredible that 46 chromosomes can divide and combine, developing into a unique human being. I pause as we visualize the heartbeat on ultrasound, understanding the innumerable steps and miracles that needed to occur to lead to this moment. I recognize the remaining miracles that will need to follow to bring a unique human into this world with their own special physical characteristics, abilities, and potential. There are so many opportunities for biological wrong turns.

The road to motherhood is a beautiful mixture of anticipation, joy, and hope. Yet for many women, this road can also be marked by profound heartache. One in four women experience this loss through miscarriage or infant loss, and yet so many carry this burden in silence. This book is a raw account by three courageous women who share their stories to offer emotional support to others who may feel alone in their loss and grief.

As a physician and woman, I am so thankful for a book that creates space for discussion, understanding, and healing. This book encourages open conversations around a topic that has often been painful and taboo. It is my hope that sharing these personal stories will foster empathy and healing for those going through similar situations. The vulnerability of these women in telling their stories will help others realize they are not alone.

DR. LESLIE ABLARD, OB-GYN
*Fellow, American College of
Obstetricians and Gynecologists*

Preface

From the bottom of our hearts and the depths of our souls, we want to start by saying we are so sorry for your loss.

We are so very sorry to be meeting you at such a difficult time in your life. What you are experiencing is hard. It's heartbreaking. It's disappointing. It's a whole mix of emotions and challenges you aren't even able to put into words.

What we want more than anything is to let you know we are here for you. We want the pages of this book to say, "We see you, we hear you, and we want to meet you at your front door and give you loving tips of healing and hope." We want to offer tips for your mental and emotional survival as well as our personal stories of loss and love. We want to not just acknowledge your loss but offer experienced words of support for surviving the most challenging aspects of grief. We want to help you survive your first days after. We want to offer insight into surviving your guilt, your depression, and the people around you—and perhaps most importantly, insight into how to survive yourself. We want these pages to be filled with compassion and understanding as well as hope as you journey with your loss.

We three women—Laurel, Kelvi, and Janelle—share a common strand in our paths of life. These are paths we didn't plan to be on, but here we are together anyway. The path we share is more than just living in the same town, having our kids go through the same school system, or shopping at the same grocery store. It's a part of each of our journeys that landed us on the daily struggle of surviving the silence of loss. The silence that has been long kept by women everywhere. The silence women dare not speak about—losing a child. The silence that women possibly still feel must be kept today. We find ourselves on that path. The path of uncomfortable, of taboo assumptions, and of expectations where it is not permissible to speak about losing a child. The place we find ourselves is in the silence of pain: the raw, gut-wrenching, life-altering, bone-weary journey of living daily without a child on Earth. A place we don't want to meet you at, but statistically speaking, we know we will. We are on the ultimate survival journey. Life without our children.

Living without Eli, Forrest, and Karaline is hard. We will not downplay that one bit. It is a wake-up-in-the-morning-and-hit-you-square-in-the-gut punch that happens over and over again. Every day, we face the reality that our children don't live with us and aren't in our care. Every day, that reality is there to greet us.

There is no one-size-fits-all solution to grief and loss. But there are survival tools that can make the pain something we can walk with.

But—and we'll say it again, *but*—we are also hit in the face every day with the opportunity to choose how we handle our grief. We choose to get up every day and walk the path we have been called to take. The path without our children physically being here. A path that is uniquely ours and ours alone. There isn't anything that makes our paths identical to anyone else's, which makes finding the perfect combination for healing the pain so personal. There is no one-size-fits-all solution to grief and loss. There is no magical combination that will lessen the burden of losing your baby or make the grief completely disappear. But there are survival tools that can make the gut-wrenching pain of a pregnancy loss something we can walk with and through daily, and yes, even talk about. The path we walk after pregnancy loss is a daily fight. One we must face, and we can face. It's a fight that is worth fighting. A fight we can boldly and bravely come into and survive.

And that's what we hope you find in this narrative of *Surviving the Silence*: three bold friends, brave women who want to meet you at your front door, walk alongside you on your path, and support you. Friends who will be bold enough to encourage you to do something so incredibly hard. We hope to encourage you to keep going down your path. We hope you find tools that help you do something "in" your grief and "with" your grief. We want to walk this path alongside you and offer insight and support. We want to help you embrace your grief and help you find JOY in the sadness. We do not want you to suffer in the silence. We pray that this book has tools to help you not only SURVIVE the silence but also THRIVE in it.

Part 1

OUR STORIES

This first part of the book contains an in-depth look into our personal paths and experiences with grief through the often-taboo topic of child loss. It contains our personal stories of losing our sweet babies. It is raw. It is real. These stories carry intimate details of our losses. They also contain the hard truths about stillbirth, miscarriage, and grief we were each faced with.

Before we begin, a word of warning: This section may not be where you need to start your path of healing. For you, this first part may be a "read as you feel ready" section. It may not be what you need right now. On your unique journey, you may find yourself heading straight into the second part of this book, where you'll find tools, advice, support, and encouragement for others who are struggling with loss.

But for us, our stories are why this book exists. This section exposes our raw hearts. It is us being bold, brave, and vulnerable, speaking words into the hard silence of loss. By baring it all, we hope to help you understand us a bit better . . . and in turn, understand yourself better. We willingly open our hearts to you to help you meet us on a personal level. And we pray that our words will resonate deeply within you.

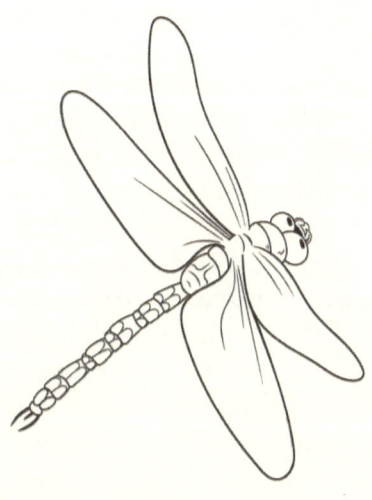

Janelle's Story

I LEANED AGAINST the edge of the counter of a high school food and consumer science classroom and began: "I was asked to come here today and share with you about pregnancy loss, miscarriage, and stillbirth."

Ugh. That statement. That sentence. Never had I dreamed of finding myself in front of a classroom of adolescents sharing such a difficult and challenging topic. Speaking words I had never planned to say, uttering a statement I never knew would need to be uttered. Shattering the silence about a topic that has become a driving force in my adult life.

Stillbirth. Pregnancy loss. Miscarriage. I was underprepared for the impact each would have in my life and the depth to which they would become a part of me. And leaning against that counter of that high school classroom, giving voice to my story, I certainly could not see what the outcome of my sharing with those high school students would bring.

Before I continue with the details of that day and the outcomes of speaking to those students, let me share some of the journey that has brought me here. My husband and I married in 2004. But before that, we grew up together. Growing up with your future spouse has many advantages and disadvantages. You see each other go through changes and challenges. You witness each other fail and succeed. You have front-row seats to some of the most embarrassing moments in each other's lives (because adolescence is like that). It's a time of growing. A time of not always being your best but working toward it. It's a time of discovery and ugliness and yet hopefulness and excitement. Seeing your soon-to-be spouse watch firsthand as you walk that part of life and then still choosing to be with you says a lot about their character and belief in you. And I am so thankful that my husband, Kirk, saw all that about me and still asked me to marry him.

We married in 2004 and, truth be told, having children was not in my comfort zone. It wasn't even on my radar of personal success for me. But, as growth and change naturally occur in life, my heart changed, and we had our first daughter, Brielle, in 2009. Everything was great. Easy, in fact. New baby. New rhythm of life. Easy (minus the colic, of course). With a new comfort zone and view of success, I now knew we were meant to be parents. Then, 2011 brought us Aleigh (pronounced "a-li"), daughter #2, lovingly nicknamed "the Beast" for good reason. She didn't sleep or eat well because she was tongue-tied. Getting back into any kind of rhythm was nearly impossible, and we were so exhausted from her never sleeping and barely eating that we began to question whether or not we really were ever supposed to be parents. But here she was, and here we were finding a new rhythm of life. So, with another new rhythm and another change in the seasons of life, Kirk and I were brave enough—or insane enough—to try for a third.

So, on Christmas Eve 2013, I took a pregnancy test and discovered we would be welcoming a third baby into our family in 2014. What a wonderful Christmas Eve church service that was, holding that secret in my heart. The excitement of a new baby. The joy of our girls becoming big sisters. Knowing that I, on the very same night that Mary had delivered her son Jesus in a manger two thousand years before, had learned that I would be welcoming a child in the year ahead was special. And the thought of sharing that news filled me with so much joy and excitement. I shared the news with Kirk as we left the candlelight service that night, and we walked hand in hand into the joy of what was to come.

Nine months is a really long time. And when you have toddlers . . . honestly, anything can feel like a really long time. But being pregnant in the summer while wrangling toddlers can feel like a really, *really* long time. Needless to say, that summer was long and hot. I found myself taking the girls on special outings all summer that year. As a public educator, I have the opportunity to be home in the summer. In preparation for that summer, I had written down ideas of fun things to do and see and share with the girls. A bucket list of ideas was written on slips of papers, sat on the kitchen island and each night, the girls would pick two slips out of the bucket and whatever was written on the slips we would do the next day. The activities included a visit to a farm. Visit a flower shop. Make a picnic lunch. Plant flowers. See dinosaurs. Go visit a college. See a beach. Quite simply, the bucket contained tons of activities to share.

What a beautiful summer it was. We had adventures to share and tons to learn. The final part of our summer even included swim lessons. It was during one of those activities that I found myself watching our three-year-old slip behind the lifeguard's back and go under the water.

She wasn't coming up.

Without hesitation, I jumped into the three-foot-deep baby pool to rescue her, my heels striking the bottom of the pool with a ton of force, and I pulled her up coughing and spitting out water.

I sat on the edge of the pool with her for a bit, thankful she was okay. I was appreciative of everyone's helpful nature. Except . . . I found myself unable to stand. I could not put weight on the bottom of my feet. I had to literally crawl on my hands and knees to get to my car. I crawled 75 yards on concrete. In July. In front of all the other nonpregnant parents. Talk about humbling.

I ended up needing an X-ray on my foot, and because I was almost nine months pregnant, there were worries and fears about radiology and my pregnancy. But despite those worries, we proceeded. I went to the hospital anyway. I was draped with some massive protective vests, and I got the X-ray.

After reading the images, the doctor called and told me that my heel was indeed fractured. I needed to be put in a boot. A large, stiff, unbending, uncomfortable, slow-me-down boot. On the bright side, I told myself, slowing down at the end of a pregnancy is probably a good thing. Right?

Slowing down is nearly impossible when you have two kids and a long list of activities you've agreed to participate in. But since my husband and I had already experienced two successful labors and deliveries since choosing to begin our family, we knew we were ready for a third. We had two beautiful, healthy baby girls delivered into the world at 8+ pounds and then 7+ pounds. I'd taken time to read all but the last few chapters in the *What to Expect When You Are Expecting* book each time. We were knowledgeable, experienced, and ready. Wrong!

And now that we were entering August and our due date of September 2, 2014, was coming closer, I needed to get some things ready at home and at school.

If you were a child of a teacher, or if you or your significant other are teachers, you likely understand the intensity and chaos of the beginning of a school year. A time for slowing down it is not. Broken heel or not, boot or no boot, August for a schoolteacher means long hours, furniture to move, labeling, coordinating, writing lessons, decorating, finishing curriculum that was put away in the spring. It's planning back-to-school nights, first-day art projects, parent night, and so, so much more. That was the start of my August in 2014—and to add to all that, I also needed to write extended lesson plans in preparation for my September 2 maternity leave. You can see how I might draw conclusions about how the words *stillbirth* and *pregnancy loss* entered my world. But in my heart and in my head, I know my work choices didn't lead to my indoctrination into stillbirth and loss.

Day after day in August was the same fast, frenzied pace, me all pregnant and in a boot. August 20 was no exception. I had told myself that I absolutely had to stay at school for our beginning-of-the-year parent meeting. I needed them to hear, from me, the year's expectations, procedures, and plans, and I needed to set the tone for the year. I told myself I couldn't slow down until certain tasks were done. I pushed myself and hustled and worked to have things prepared for everyone else. So the transition would move forward smoothly.

But the thing is, I hadn't felt the baby move for a while. I even mentioned it to colleagues earlier that morning. It wasn't on the forefront of mind as I busily worked through the days. I hadn't thought about the possibility of problems in a pregnancy at 38 weeks. Admittedly I didn't ever make it to the last few chapters of the *What to Expect When You're Expecting* book. Why would I? After the first trimester, the success rate of healthy deliveries is exponentially higher. I didn't worry. I didn't read it. I didn't ask about it. I just assumed all would be okay.

At the end of that long, chaotic August day, after the parent meeting that I made myself power through, I finally came home that night around 8:30 p.m. and drank a huge, caffeinated pop in hopes to jump-start some baby kicks. If you have ever experienced these kicks, you know what I am talking about. The soft flutters, hard jabs, and even tiny heels pushing up under your rib cage are feelings that you count on and look forward to. I didn't feel those. I didn't feel anything but heaviness in the same spot I had been feeling heavy over the last day or so. Almost like I needed to physically move the baby from one side of my uterus to the other.

After telling my husband I wasn't sure if the baby was okay, I went to lie down in bed. After an hour of rest, I came downstairs in tears and said,

"I think we need to go to the hospital." I just wanted to reassure myself that everything was fine, but part of me really didn't want to go because I didn't want to be a bother to the nurses or doctors for a false alarm or some unwarranted worry. (A side note about me is that I struggle with feeling like I am being a bother to others, even today.) But my husband insisted, and we went to the hospital anyway.

We arrived at our local ER, and with the doppler they had access to, they tried to find a heartbeat. Tried to find a heartbeat. Tried to find . . . a heartbeat. Bless their hearts, the on-call doctor herself was pregnant, and she kept reiterating that she wasn't great with using a doppler. She stated something along the lines of "the doppler isn't used all that much in our small, local clinic." See, our small town has a population of about 3,000. She wanted to call over to the hospital in Salina, a town of about 45,000 people, and talk to the OB-GYN there. So, the doctor left the ER room and called the hospital in Salina to tell them we were on our way over to labor and delivery, at 38 weeks pregnant, and that she wasn't sure if there was a heartbeat.

With unplanned deliveries, you typically get whoever is on call, and it just so happened, the doctor on call that night was my preferred OB-GYN. Seriously, only God can do something like that.

As we got into our car to make the short-but-long drive, I still wasn't realizing the outcome of our first hospital stop when we got in the car. My husband and I held hands as he drove us the 40 miles over to Salina. I cried a lot. At this point, nothing had been definitely confirmed, so I was still silently hoping that everything was okay. Trying to make myself believe that the doppler and the doctors were wrong. My husband made that drive holding my hand; I was holding that silent hope in my heart even as the tears streaming down my face foretold what was to come.

It's difficult to put into words what we were experiencing; an out-of-body experience may sum it up. It's a feeling where you are present but not fully present. You're in the moment, yet so far removed.

Kirk and I walked into the ER and were checked in by this wonderfully-excited-for-us receptionist. She was very bubbly, super happy and full of energy and questions. She wanted to know if this was our first child. We said no, it's our third. She said something along the lines of "Maybe that's why you're so calm." . . . Calm? Really? In hindsight, we probably seemed that way to her. But in reality, we were probably in shock. There were some more pleasantries and a huge congratulations before we were escorted up to the elevator. If that wasn't an uncomfortable encounter—and to no fault of the receptionist—I don't know what is. I looked pregnant because I was all but ready to pop, so her being excited for us made sense to her. But for us, that was hard.

It's difficult to put into words what we were experiencing; an out-of-body experience may sum it up. Physically, we were sitting in an exam room on the sixth floor of the hospital, but mentally and emotionally, we weren't there. It's a feeling where you are present but not fully present. You're in the moment, yet so far removed. It's so hard to believe what is going on that you actually don't believe it.

That's where we were when our doctor came in with a sonogram machine. He placed it on my pregnant belly and scanned and scanned and waited and waited and waited. It was the longest ten minutes of my life

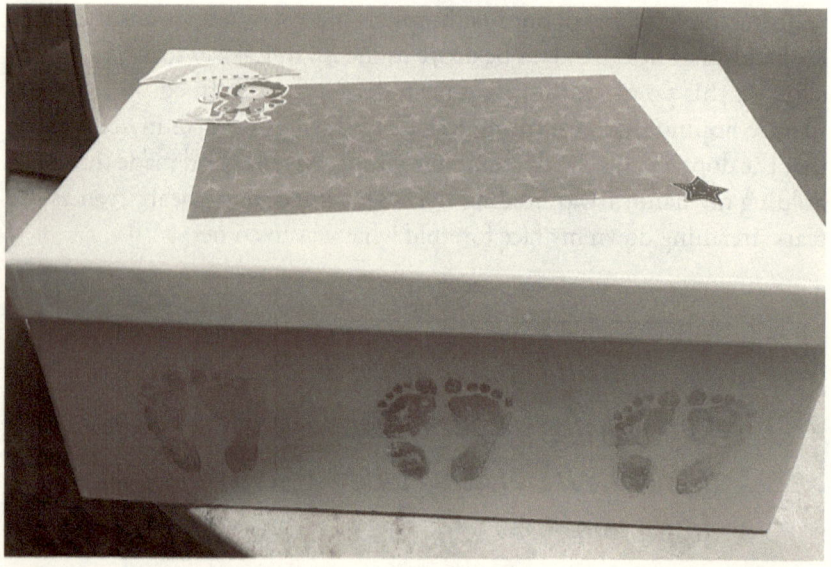

"Eli's box"—given to Janelle by the hospital to hold treasured items to remember him

before the doctor removed the gelled paddle and shook his head no. No heartbeat. No movement. No hope. That's all he could do. He just shook his head. The nurse just stood there, looking at us, and my tears continued to come. Those tears that had been falling since the car ride. Those tears that had foretold what was to come, even when I couldn't and didn't want to believe it was possible. Those tears knew that our baby was gone.

We'd lost our baby. Full-term. Twelve days away from the intended due date of September 2.

The doctor couldn't speak. He had already walked alongside us for two healthy pregnancies. He had delivered one of our two girls. His typically boisterous personality changed at that moment so it seemed. I couldn't imagine what he was going through or how many other mothers or families he'd walked this road with. All I knew was that our baby was gone and none of us had answers. I couldn't really do much or think much. But what I did do was repeat over and over and over again, during that long ultrasound and throughout the next day of hard decisions was the phrase "We're not the first and we won't be the last."

"We're not the first and we won't be the last . . ." Only God knew why that particular statement was all I could utter when we didn't hear that tiny heartbeat. Maybe sharing it with you is the only reason that phrase came to me in the labor and delivery room. Maybe it's that I want to assure the next woman, "You're not the first"—not in a mean and hurtful way, but to share with you that many strong women before you have felt what you felt or are feeling. Those women have hurt like you have hurt. I have hurt like you are hurting.

That is why we want to meet you at the front door of your journey and be there for you. I, for one, want to knock on your door and be there for you so that when the next woman's turn comes, you'll be there on her doorstep to help her. Because we are not the last. We are not the last ones who will lose a child. And until the statistic of 1 out of every 4 women suffering loss at some level is lessened or becomes none, we women need to keep showing up for each other. We have to show up willing to be raw. Willing to be real. We need to be able to speak truth and comfort to those who so desperately need it. We need to not hide this crazy mess of emotions in a closet. This intense grief is not something that fits inside the little white box you carry out of the hospital either. It's something so much more. So much deeper.

It wasn't until that little white box came into the hospital room that I understood how complicated the battle, both religious and political, over identifying and labeling life really was. My little boy, Eli Douglas, was delivered—not born—at 4:35 p.m. on August 21, 2014. He was delivered still into the hands of a nurse. Cesarean was not an option as it is considered a major surgery and wasn't medically warranted. And trust me—I asked for something easier. I didn't want to have to go through the physical pain of vaginal delivery. But vaginal delivery it would be. The doctor sat in our room for a little while to talk through the next steps in this process. I can't say that I remember much of this conversation. It was part of that "here but not really here" feeling. The doctor planned to induce labor with Pitocin and encouraged me to get an epidural so I could be as comfortable as possible.

I had to lie in that hospital bed from 11:00 p.m. to 4:35 p.m. the next day going through all the labor phases—the epidural, the tightening of my uterus, the contractions intensifying and coming closer and closer together—all the while knowing that I would not be coming home with the gift of a child. Oh, those tears just kept coming. I cried because the crib was already made up. The clothes were all washed and folded. The changing table and toys had been sorted and set up in the living room awaiting the arrival of baby #3. And yet, I wasn't going to bring a baby home. Not for myself. For my husband. Not for our daughters. Or to our folks—they, too, would be experiencing this great loss at different levels. None of us would be able to skirt the hardness of loss. So all day that day, I simply cried.

LABOR AND DELIVERY is just that: labor. It is strength. It is pain. It is mind over matter. It is intense. And yet women endure this pain daily and then sometimes have to walk away empty-armed when they lose a baby. I didn't quite understand the ache in my arms. The emptiness. The heaviness. That feeling didn't hit right away. It came somewhere in the second week of being home without Eli. It came when the rush of fast decisions and the slow trickle of visitors started to happen. It came when instead of returning to the classroom, I was home alone on maternity leave without a baby. Much of what I do recall only came from the many journals and pages and notes and memos I started writing for myself. I couldn't remember anything during that time. Seriously, my mind couldn't remember *anything*. I still have missing moments and events from that time. My brain just shut down, and I lived on God and emotions and the strength of others. I let come what needed to come. I pushed all the unimportant stuff out of my head and worked solely on surviving.

Many days, I felt like I was failing. And I was, to an extent. I was failing at something daily. I'd take a drive and cry the whole time. Then when I stopped the car, I couldn't muster enough strength to drive home. I'd call a friend and tell them just how dark it was around me and that I was completely lost. I'd call someone to talk me out of the darkness. I'd sit down in what we joked was my "contraction chair" at home. This was the chair I chose to sit in through the lengthy contractions I experienced throughout my whole pregnancy. I would sit in that chair and write about the hurt and the anger. Oh, I was angry. Mad that Eli was gone. Mad that I couldn't just be the "before" me. Mad at things people said. And the longing was there too. The desperate plea for all of it to be different. I wrote. And I wrote. And I wrote. I wrote everything—the hate, the pleading with God. I wrote his name—Eli. I wrote my thoughts and feelings. Everything. I wrote. And I read too. I was working hard so life could become easier. Because that's how I viewed these days and these moments. There were easy hours and hard hours. Easy days and hard days. Eventually there were two easy days together, but then there would be another wave of back-to-back hard days that would crash down on me. Nothing was linear. Nothing flowed. Every time I'd feel like I could step forward into the light, I'd step back into some other darkness. Darkness that could apparently even come from distant future loss. The loss of our son in a football jersey with our last name on it . . . gone. Carrying on my husband's bloodline and family name . . . gone. All the firsts we would have with him . . . gone. See, Eli was our firstborn son. And I was now carrying the loss and pressure of all that. My husband and his family never put any of that on me—it was all self-inflicted. And that was hard.

Those dark times were debilitating. They could stop me in my tracks.

Those were the hard days. All days, no matter the outcome, were never "good" or "bad" for me; they were "easy" and "hard." And mostly, they were just hard! Throughout my life, I have worked to believe there is always good. God is good, and even when life is hard—He is present and things can be good. God has made a way for us to enter into His goodness. But we have to do the work. We have to choose to walk into His presence, into His light. And at those times when life is exceedingly hard and full of overwhelming days, we may even have to crawl—down on our bellies if necessary—painstakingly inch our way forward to see the light that is always there. We may have to crawl to get there. But we have to do the work. We have to grieve. We have to heave heavy sobs. We have to circle back through memories and emotions and feelings. Start over, step back, rest, retry, and reimagine what life is now.

And for me, life was now hard.

THE WEEKS PASSED, and I had finally returned to work. On one of my hard days, I sat bawling in the conference room, and a colleague came in to be with me. She, too, had suffered loss, and while we sat there, I asked if she felt changed because of her loss. Had what she'd been through made her different? Had it set her on a new path of life? And her answer to me was, "Not really." No? Unchanged? She was the same? How is that possible? As I thought through how I felt, I realized that my answer was different than hers. Yes, I am different. Yes, I am changed. Yes, this grief that happened in me and to me has changed my core. I am not the same me as I was before we lost Eli. While that's hard to process, I know that being different is okay. It shows me that where I was and what I was doing was no longer the path I was called to, and that God was shaping me for something new.

I didn't know it at the time, but the change started back in the hospital room with my utterance, "We're not the first and we won't be the last." My desire is to help others. My desire is to find those lost mommas and reach out to them. I have slowed down my physical and mental pace. I have intentionally made the effort to take notice of nature, books, society, and love. Colors are different. Time is different. And I see dragonflies, butterflies, and growth everywhere I look.

Dragonflies and butterflies are Eli's messages to our family. They are the signs and symbols that my heart, without planning, notices, captures, and takes in. They arrive when my heart needs them most, and always in an "only God can" way. Like a dragonfly perched on the end of a fishing pole three days after labor and delivery with Eli while my husband's buddies took him and the girls fishing to help pass some time. Or a butterfly actually landing on my shoulder while out at recess or working in our stone yard on the outskirts of Ellsworth. They show up painted on the side of buildings, on everything from backpacks and notebooks to cards and keychains from loss groups. Dragonflies and butterflies are our symbolic point of connection to him. They are that tangible symbol that makes a way for my heart to feel what I can no longer see. They give me a moment to pause and reflect. To slow down and be. And . . . to be in that moment with God, the giver of life.

Eli never came into the world with life, but there was so much life in him. He enjoyed a lifetime of experiences that summer when the girls and I took activity papers out of our jar each night. He had a heartbeat inside of me. So much life. His kicks, stretches, and heartbeat during the pregnancy were so strong I'd have to sit in my contraction chair to get through those early Braxton-Hicks contractions. He had so much life that sometimes those contractions were intense enough to stop me in my tracks and I'd have to sit. After losing him, that chair became a position of comfort for me. A place in which I could feel him again. I felt every part of his life while sitting in that spot. And while my body failed him and at times I even feel like I have survivor's guilt, it wasn't anything in my control. But I felt those feelings—just like I felt him move. It wasn't anything I did or didn't do. At least that's what I have to tell myself to remember that I am not the one the world revolves for. God is. And in His greatness and my weakness, I cannot control the story He is living through me. It is His story.

Eli is God's story in me. A testimony to God's character and strength, to His love and joy and mercies. Eli is a blessing from God. A blessing to my family and to those who know his story.

There is a song—"Blessings" by Laura Story—that has become an anthem for me. It speaks of our great disappointments and the aching of this life. It includes words about revealing a thirst this world can't satisfy. I know that I cannot be satisfied here on Earth. I am made for something more than flesh and bone. Eli was made for more than Earth. And the tears that I shed for him, that our friends and family shed for him, are actually mercies. Mercies from our Creator. The song goes on to speak that our greatest disappointments can actually provide healing and our trials can actually be blessings. We cannot be satisfied on Earth. Our home is not here on Earth. There are no truer words than the words of this song that could describe how I felt as I struggled through losing Eli. My trials are blessings so long as I choose to view them that way. And that my home is not here on Earth but in Heaven. And Eli's home wasn't with us either. It was and is with Jesus.

BACK TO THAT NIGHT when the doctors found no heartbeat and we delivered Eli still. We left the hospital only three hours after a full-term delivery. Three hours. The hospital staff sure can get you out of there quickly when things aren't "normal."

I didn't understand the depth of the pain that would hit me when we returned home. That night, I cried. I bawled. All night long. I shook. I sobbed. My husband cradled me all night long and rubbed my back, trying to express his understanding. But he, too, was silent. The pain he felt was enormous. He didn't even have words to help himself, much less me. Eventually, I fell asleep, completely exhausted from what happened—only to be woken with the pain of my uterus recoiling, trying to contract back to a normal size. Then to be woken again with the need to change my ice packs and pads. And again to be woken with the tightening in my breasts.

The female body doesn't know that its baby isn't in need of milk. The female body only knows that it needs to provide for what it has been carrying for months. The female body is prepared to complete its entire mission, even when you don't need it to. There is no pill to take to dry up your milk ducts. Again, trust me, I asked. There is no quick way to keep the "letdown" of the milk from coming. No pill to dry it up and make it go away. I just stuffed cabbage leaves in my bra and prayed that no one hugged me. The crunch of the cabbage leaves was embarrassing to explain to others. I spent two weeks not wanting to hug anyone but having to make contact as some people need an embrace to show their support. Everyone wants to express their sympathy and sadness to you at a time like this, but your chest is full of milk and you don't want it to come out. So you avoid hugs, or you decide to take cold showers and use a couple of heads of cabbage and wait about two weeks before that specific "new mother body change" dissipates. Eli wasn't our first baby, so I was very much aware of witch hazel and ice pads, squirt bottles, sprays, and patting dry—all the while still peeing my pants when I bent over, coughed, or sneezed. So when all of those female body changes came, they were more reminders of what didn't come. And every one of those changes triggered one of the many components of grief. Anger. Sadness. Confusion . . .

And what was it that didn't come: a sweet, 6 lb. 15 oz., 21 in. long baby boy. There were no giggles or gas or rolling or smiles. There wasn't anything that you'd typically get with a newborn. We received sympathy cards and condolences instead. People would stop in and want to hear the story. They'd deliver casseroles, flowers, and paper products. All wonderful expressions of love and support, yet heartbreaking for us. All things I didn't know I needed to allow people to do for us. Mostly, it helped them grieve. It helped them connect with us. It brought them closure. That's why people come. They need to help. They need you to know they care. So allowing people to stop by helped them.

I am not wired to ask for help, want help, or feel comfortable accepting help. I'm a broken person, I know. But through this journey, I have learned that accepting "help" allows others to grieve with you. It doesn't show weakness on your part. It opens a door to allow people to connect with you in a way that is healing for them as it is for you. Opening yourself to allowing others to support and encourage you and offer their sympathy changes your perspective of what it means to show hospitality. As one of the disciplines of Christianity, hospitality is a part of spiritual growth. When you invite others in, they share the innermost areas of your "home." They witness you where you are comfortable and where you let your guard down. Having a hospitable spirit allows others to be a part of you and your calling. It makes you vulnerable. And vulnerable is not something that is easy for many of us to be.

I was completely vulnerable for eighteen months. I cried so much. I got lost driving. Sometimes I had no idea how I made it to the next town or even where I was driving to. I didn't wear makeup. I wore black clothing. I couldn't eat supper. I couldn't pay bills. Yes, there were months in which we forgot to pay our water bill. And by the grace of God and the kindness of strangers, it would be paid in full by the time I got around to it. I openly wrote on social media how the days and months were being marked. I shared my heart's pain and loss. One month: One boy. One tiny heart. Two months: Two feet. Two hands. Three . . . and so on. I was vulnerable to the heartache of the first baptism back in the church. The baptism that should have been Eli's but wasn't. I wept. I then would stay home from church at times, just to avoid having to reimagine what didn't happen or hear the sound of another infant crying, which would make my arms ache and the tears roll.

God is beyond merciful.
We just have to choose to see it that way.

Witnessing the first baptism at church wasn't the only hole that needed to be patched. There was the birth of my best friend's little one and my first return to the labor and delivery wing of a hospital. I sat in that hospital room holding her beautiful baby, who was just perfect at 6 lb. 15 oz. Yes, the exact same weight as Eli—another "only God can do that" moment. Only He can patch a hole that needs patching. God is so amazing. He can bring to life, in your best friend, a baby whose weight so closely matches the one you lost—just two months later—that when you hold them, it's as if your arms remember. That weight helps to heal. God is beyond merciful. We just have to choose to see it that way.

Seeing situations through God's eyes helped us on our journey of welcoming in others and being vulnerable. It comforted us when we put away the baby clothes and took apart the crib. Yes, those things had to be done, partly because the doctor had said we should wait at least six weeks before having intercourse or even considering another baby. But I didn't want any other child. Some days, I didn't even want to get out of bed. Choosing to see these hard moments through God's perspective kept Kirk and me close as we met with the funeral home to make plans for the burial of our baby.

Back in the delivery room, when Eli was delivered at 4:35 p.m., the nurse asked us if we wanted to know what gender the baby was. I hadn't even thought about *not* knowing the gender of our baby. Kirk and I have always liked waiting to find out. The nine full months of guessing and conversations with others about what we thought the baby was made the wait exciting. For us, those moments made being slightly underplanned when the baby finally arrived worth it. So, when the nurse asked if we wanted to know, of course we said yes. She looked at both of us and said, "It looks like a little boy."

Oh, my heart! My tears fell harder. Hard, eye-swelling tears. That's when I fully realized my dreams and plans for bringing home a baby were gone, because the delivery room was absolutely silent. Nothing came after the nurse's words. No crying, no rushing about with doctors, no hearing specialists, no weighing and measuring. No bath. No social security number documents. Nothing normal. Nothing expected. Just the ticking of the clock. I can still hear the clock.

The nurse covered our baby in a knitted cap and swaddling blanket, then handed me a tiny bundle. Heavy yet so light. Unmoving. Eyes closed. Lips sealed in red. A button nose, just like his sister, and soft cheeks that when I leaned in to kiss them were cold. Cold enough that that feeling lingered for days and weeks after. The coolness of his skin would leave me with nightmare-like reminders that I could still feel.

Eli was born still. With blackened fingernails and toenails. With wisps of blond hair. With no visible sign of distress, other than the damage on his forehead from pushing.

IN HINDSIGHT, ELI had most likely been gone for two days prior to our first ER trip to our small-town clinic. Being a schoolteacher, I had told myself that I could slow down after the room was set and I had the parent meeting. I just *had* to have that parent meeting—mostly because I didn't realize that things can go wrong during any phase of a pregnancy. I truly did not know that loss could happen at any time. Once I got through the first trimester and told everyone we were expecting, I didn't know that I could still lose our little one. That possibility is covered in the last few chapters in the *What to Expect* book, but I never finished the book, so I didn't learn everything I could have or should have.

Because Eli had been "gone" prior to delivery, our time window of being with Eli was short. His little body couldn't handle being loved on and held for long. His mouth and eyes started to seep. We held him for thirty minutes, each of us. Kirk standing there at the window holding his firstborn son, tears slowly coming down his cheeks. Me with tears pouring down my face, just holding him, holding the special blanket we had purchased for him on his cheek so that when I left the hospital, I'd still have something that had touched his skin.

The nurses then took him to clean him up a bit. Prior to all of the hardness that came from the time we entered the hospital until watching him leave with the nurse, we had been overwhelmed with the questions about what we were going to do with his body. Were we going to take him home in "the box," leave him in the hospital to dispose of, or call the funeral home? Were we going to take pictures of him and with him? Did we want an autopsy? If we were going to call the funeral home, did we want him embalmed? And if not, did we know that we wouldn't want to see his body again? And if we planned on a funeral, how did we want to announce it? Who would be allowed to come? Did we want our pastor there? What did we want the obituary to say?

These questions all came after the initial shock of knowing Eli would be delivered without a breath and were accompanied with the hospital's stillbirth packet including information from Now I Lay Me Down to Sleep photography and about the reality of postpartum depression on a mother of loss. It contained a phone number to a local pastor and but nothing in that pack eased the deep sadness that was growing in me.

We kept Eli near us for three hours. But we could tell it was time to let him go. His body was weak and so were my emotions. The nurses washed him and clothed him in the only outfit we had with us: a gray-and-white elephant onesie. Not knowing we were having a boy, and not having shopped much before the baby was to arrive, we took a gifted outfit from a dear friend and laid our boy to rest in it. The knit hat donated to the hospital remained on his head, but his little feet were bare. The nurses brought

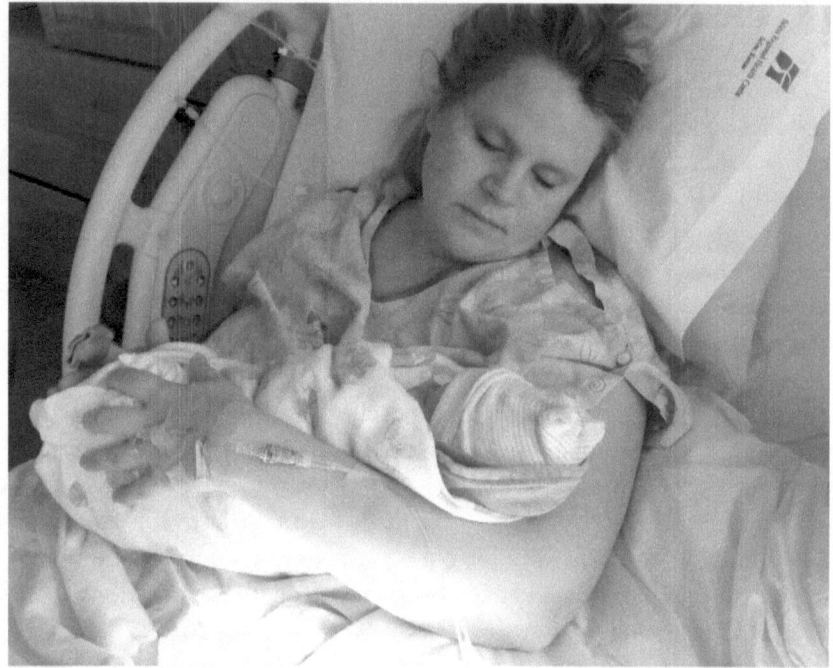

Janelle cradling Eli just after delivering him into the world still

Eli back to us for one final moment: all dressed, all bundled, all ready to be carried out of the labor and delivery room. Oh, how it hurt to watch the funeral home attendant walk out the door with that bundle. Then Eli was gone, and I was still stuck in the delivery bed waiting to shower and put on my "new mother" gear. I was angry. I was hurt. I was present but not really. I was so many things.

We were able to leave about an hour after Eli, and that long, silent drive home was another reminder of the hospital room that Eli came into. Silent.

MY EYES HURT so bad for days. They were puffy and full and painful to open. I cried so much those first three days that I ran out of tears at times. Visitors were asked not to come to the house for a few days just to give us some time to attempt to process what was going on. No one but Eli's grandparents and the pastor were invited to attend his burial. That was yet another hard decision. You can't unsee something once it's been seen. And that little box sitting on top of the burial table is etched in my mind. It's not a visual I wish on anyone, let alone my siblings and nieces and nephews. I sat on a cold metal chair during the last bit of August and can still feel the cool of the metal through my black dress. It was the only dress I have owned or worn since my wedding day: another day that also changed and shaped my life. I sat on that metal chair as the pastor to my left led our small group in prayer and Scripture. The whole time, I was holding on to three roses, yellow and white in color, and the blanket Eli was intended to snuggle with as an infant. We were the only two plots in that back row of the cemetery at that time. Empty and unguarded. Open and alone. All things a baby should not feel or be. But here he was, alone in the cemetery.

As we finished our service, my dad led us all in an unexpected singing of the doxology:

> *"Praise God from whom all blessings flow,*
> *Praise him all creatures here below*
> *Praise him above ye heavenly host*
> *Praise Father, Son, and Holy Ghost.*
> *Amen."*

We left the cemetery and returned to family members making sure our girls were being cared for and loved. Our pastor advised us to make a decision about who should be in attendance because her remarks on losing a child would be different depending on the group. We had to make hard decisions in a hard and dark time in life. Had I prepared, I may have allowed aunts and uncles and nieces and nephews to come and to allow our girls to be present in the final farewell. We might have allowed grandparents to come into the hospital and hold Eli. But what we did was done in love for everyone. Not selfishly but definitely done with protection and love in mind. Neither my parents, nor Kirk's, ever got to meet Eli.

Remembering back to that August 21st day, my folks had made a mad rush to town to bring clothing and necessities to my husband and I as we awaited our delivery time. They sat in that hospital room with us for a while. I can't even remember if anything was said, but I sure felt like a disappointment to them. It was hard to have them look at me from across the room. They didn't share their wishes or hopes, and I couldn't really say anything at all. Honestly, I just hoped they would leave so I wouldn't have to face them. I faintly remember our pastor making a visit to our room as well and offering a prayer for us, but I was not welcoming. And I sure wasn't wearing the mask I've worked so hard to build and use to protect myself from others' thoughts and opinions of me. The mask that I spent thirty-two years creating. I think at one point I even avoided talking to everyone. I just closed myself off and honestly just tried to remember to breathe.

Since we started to have kids, my husband and I have always agreed on the surprise delivery. No gender reveal, no planned induction. And no planned induction meant a surprise call to our loved ones and friends when the baby finally decided to arrive. So early that next morning, we started to make phone calls, one of which needed to be to my school's district office. The phone call started with their presumed congratulations, but I had to utter something about the baby not breathing. I had nothing but tears and feelings of withdrawal. Having to tell my superintendent the baby was born still and knowing that not only my current class but the previous students who had been a part of my nine-month journey would be told by him the hard news was more than I could stomach that morning. My best friends at school having to be consoled and even walked out of class throughout the day because the tears and heartache wouldn't stop for them either made me want to cry. All of those thoughts were so heavy to hold and I wanted to just shut off my feelings. Phone calls to family members—who answered the phone all giddy and excited and teasing, only to be stopped in their tracks with my tears and the choking out of the words "there's no heart-beat"—have put a strain on some of those relationships still today. So many relationships have changed. Some deepened. Some disappeared. None of these changes were intentional but all were products of the situation.

Close friends came and sat with me in the quiet of my maternity leave, offering a listening ear or a Coke. Time. They needed some time with me, and I needed some time with my "Eli things." Like Coca-Cola—the one thing that would keep the morning sickness at bay during my whole pregnancy with Eli. It became a way to remember him. The over 500 cards shared and memorials gifted and presented in Eli's name. All things that helped me heal. All things that helped other people reach out. There was a bracelet with the birthstones of all three of my kids. Journaling notebooks with dragonflies on the cover. A necklace with a foot engraved with Eli's name. So many more items that mean the world to me.

I had weekly visits with my pastor in an effort to find some understanding of what God had allowed into my life. Our focus included much of what it is that we should "put on" daily as a Christian and much more about the depths of love. Man, do I love that boy. To grieve so deeply must mean there was that much love.

Even with all these beautiful tokens, after getting home and trying to find a new balance/rhythm, I found myself missing the idea of shopping for baby clothes and needing some Eli items I had decided upon myself. Shopping for clothes was a desire that stirred in my heart, so I went. I drove myself back to Salina, crying the whole way. I walked through Target's baby boy section and cried. I touched all the soft blankets and looked through all the "baby brother" shirts, the whole time feeling crushed and lonely. Wanting what I couldn't have. Knowing that I was probably a spectacle that others wondered about. But there I was in the boy section, longing for a son and the chance to buy him clothes. So I bought an outfit, knowing he'd never wear it but needing something to ease my pain. Needing something in the color blue. Not pink, not yellow, and not even the gray he was laid in the casket in. Knowing that I had lost my boy was a hurt that ran deep. It seeped into my bones.

I visited the cemetery every day. Every day! For eleven months. It didn't matter the time of day or night. I'd walk out on people and events, including the first Thanksgiving at my folks' house. I *needed* to go to the cemetery. I needed to be close to Eli. The cemetery had always been an extremely uncomfortable place for me. Cold and final. I hated to visit them while growing up, and here I was, an adult of 32, finding a "home" there. From the purchasing of an additional burial plot—three, in fact—to the burial service for Eli, I found myself being called to them. Called to the cemetery. The stillness of the mornings, just like the hospital delivery room, to the beautiful sunrises and pink-and-blue-colored sunsets. My heart was drawn to lying on the grass by the mound of dirt, bare and bladeless. I sat on my knees many days just crying. Trying to find words to pray. Words that would take the pain away. And none ever came. I just kept showing up.

That first early morning in the cemetery was maybe the reason I kept coming back. It was the first and only time I heard Eli in my mind. He said, "I'm okay, Mom"—and I replied, "I know, buddy. I know." Hearing that phrase, whether it was allowed by God, a desire of my soul, or just my mind playing tricks, I heard him and felt a bit of relief. Knowing that he was and is still connected to me here on Earth. That even as a tiny baby lost in this world, he has a voice in Heaven.

WE BURIED ELI three days after his delivery. I can still see the empty row in the cemetery. I can see the line of evergreens making a wind block in the distance. Even today, ten years later, I can still see that tiny box lying on the table ready to be lowered into the earth. And even today, there is still only a small indentation in the ground. A constant reminder that a small burial box was placed in the ground, now below a carved limestone marker with the letter *E* that Eli's dad hand-chiseled for his son. A small memorial stone that now rests to the left of my husband's and my plots.

To the depths of my soul, I ached for this sweet boy. I ached for what should have been. I withdrew from things. That ache turned into anger and frustration. Anger at myself and my body for killing my child. Anger at my job for the unintentional yet real expectation of not allowing myself to choose myself over others. Frustrated at God for allowing this in my life, for calling this to be part of my story. Frustrated that I couldn't pull myself out of this dark hole that had me spiraling. On top of that, I was angry that my maternity leave was just about over. Those six weeks were flying by at this point and the thought of going back to work to continue to support my family was heavy on my mind.

I had spent much of those six weeks visiting the cemetery, sitting alone in my contraction chair, having friends stop by to offer comfort and support, journaling, and openly following the emotional mayhem of my conscience and subconscious. The extreme swing of emotions that come with loss and miscarriage are powerful. Some days, I was consolable. A good cry while holding Eli's blankies allowed me to get up and attempt to cook dinner or help with preschool homework for my oldest. Other days, a good cry turned into a confused and angry outburst at my own mother, telling her to leave me alone and never come back to my house. Then there were other days when the grief roller coaster had me incapable of getting out of bed to even get dressed. And at the time, I didn't know that letting the emotions come and go as they pleased—honoring them as I felt them—was actually helping to heal my heart. In the middle of those swings, it sure didn't feel like it helped, but allowing what I was feeling to take priority in the easy and the hard moments was essential for my healing. God does that for us too. He heals us.

I wish I could say that after six weeks of leave and the roller coaster of emotions, I was healed, but that would be untrue. I went back to work a broken person. Back to the same room and the same job and the same expectations that I had prioritized instead of Eli. The same place where I lost this baby. I found that I was beginning to resent the profession I was working in. Teaching is a passion profession, and my focus was on others instead of my own baby.

Nevertheless, I went back to my classroom and failed daily and weekly at trying to put in an eight-hour day of tending to the needs and wants and issues of others (many, in my eyes, being less than important in the grand scheme of things). I showed up, but it was far from my best performance. Wearing makeup just wasn't important anymore; my eyes were still so swollen from crying I couldn't put any on, or it just felt like too much effort. I skipped dressing up for Halloween for my students because I didn't have it in me. I'd start a day or lesson and end up stepping across the hall and asking a colleague to cover for me so I could go to the break room and finish crying. But I just kept showing up in that classroom for those long eight-hour days even though my "best performance" was unattainable. Frankly, I *was* changed. And I *am* changed. I don't teach like I did before. I don't prioritize like I did before. I don't love like I did before. And I sure don't live like I did before. Now I live waiting for Heaven to come.

Kirk and I have always lived for more. We have lived for God. We have put ourselves in the hands of something bigger. So when we realized that our journey would include making hard decisions about when we might want to go through pregnancy again, we knew we could only "let go and let God." We'd have to let God have control. So, after losing Eli, we gave our hearts some much-needed healing time. And after two years, we tried to conceive again. God willing, we would have another child to welcome into our family.

Fast-forward to September 2016. I had decided to take a pregnancy test after what I thought was a missed cycle. And sure enough, it showed two lines. Pregnant! We were elated. And worried. And nervous, yet hopeful. We were ready to "let God." It was volleyball season, and that weekend, I was headed to Abilene to help coach a yearly tournament that our freshmen girls played in. So I secretly told the head coach that I was pregnant. She was beyond excited for me. She made sure I knew that if I ever needed anything, I should just let her know.

After our first match of the day, I headed to the restroom and noticed some bleeding. I told myself to be calm and not panic. I told myself to stay focused and trust God's plan. I headed out to coach matches two and three. While our day wasn't overly intense, I still felt uneasy and certain I knew what was happening inside my body. I was almost numb to the idea that this, again, was our calling in life. I returned home from coaching and shared with Kirk what I thought was going on. We waited through the weekend and called our OB-GYN for that early ultrasound on Monday. But I knew. In fact, I was certain of it. We were going through another loss.

You know silence. It happens in several different places in life. Like when you are hiking on a secluded trail. Or the silence that comes with freshly fallen snow. But the silence that comes from the ultrasound room is a whole different silence. The sonographer says nothing. They just roll that doppler over your belly and type into their computer. They can't tell you anything. But you know. And they know. And that's exactly what we found to be happening for us in 2016. We had a positive pregnancy test, noticed the bleeding, and then experienced the silence of the ultrasound room. After being sent to the doctor and hearing him confirm that there was no heartbeat yet again, we felt lost and broken and behind. Behind in starting a new family and lost in what we thought we were called to do: parent another child. We had nothing to bring home again. Our arms were empty.

How does a person deal with something like this? Deal with another heartbreaking loss? Deal with a death? Deal with grief about what should be? Deal with hate and sadness? How were we going to do all that work again? Yet here we were, stepping into another level of loss. This child, too, was gone too soon. Such disappointment.

After the doctor confirmed that this baby was lost too, we were told that going through a home loss was the next step. I would need to pass this fetus as a D&C wasn't necessary. That, too, was awful. It was hard. Two days later, on a Wednesday night, I lay in the fetal position on the couch, having contractions. I made frequent trips to the bathroom, hoping and praying the pain would stop but yet willing to go through all of that to be able to keep this baby. But there was nothing I could do. This baby was gone too. It was a long night of lying on the living room sofa with my girls and husband nearby. With uterine contractions coming. Intensifying. Knowing my body was dispelling the remnants of what should have been our fourth child. Here I was. Vulnerable. Losing another baby. In front of my family. My body was failing this baby too. I found myself in a deep, dark spot. Again. Hate. Pain. Anguish. Old feelings resurfacing, but wanting to hold another baby all the same.

We lost that baby in the fall at about 7 weeks' gestation. Two years after losing Eli. We felt so certain God had called us to be parents again, but here we were, surviving another loss.

So what do you do when you are uncertainly certain of a call on your life? You wait. You wait for another blessing to come your way. And it did. In November of 2016, we had another positive pregnancy test. A gift. A chance at redemption. A chance to heal on a different level. We were expecting a baby and praying that all would be well this time. Callen joined our family on September 18th, 2017. He was a turning point. An opportunity to live again. To enjoy more joy. To step forward. Callen didn't replace Eli, but he was a huge part of our healing. Eli will *always* be missing. He will *always* be our firstborn son. He will *always* be missed. But Callen brought joy and peace and a new level of trust. We found that we had to trust God's timing.

And God's timing brought us not only Callen but in 2020, an unexpected surprise. Another pregnancy—unplanned. While I'd like to say Kirk and I had worked out all our doubts in God's timing and provision, that would be a lie. As humans, we fall short, so when this pregnancy came along, our trust was sometimes hesitant and riddled with doubt. How could we do this? Why was this happening? What are we supposed to do now? These were all questions we asked ourselves. We'd already been through two losses. Could we go through all the emotions of losing a third child?

With nights full of tears, as well as this newfound joy that now wavered as weeks turned into months and the months turned into the final trimester, we could only wonder what was to become of this. After experiencing "fetal demise" (yes, that's what it's called in the medical literature), the prenatal visits at the end of term change. There are more check-ins. You're being watched more closely, monitored more closely. All these changes occurred with Callen's delivery too, but they intensified even more now that this delivery was a "geriatric pregnancy." Each thing was a mix of worry and trust.

As our journey led into the last month of this unexpected blessing, I went in for a weekly check and my blood pressure was high—so high I was sent to the ER to deliver immediately.

With no bag packed, no car seat ready, and still work to do at school, the delivery process began. I got pumped full of magnesium and then Pitocin

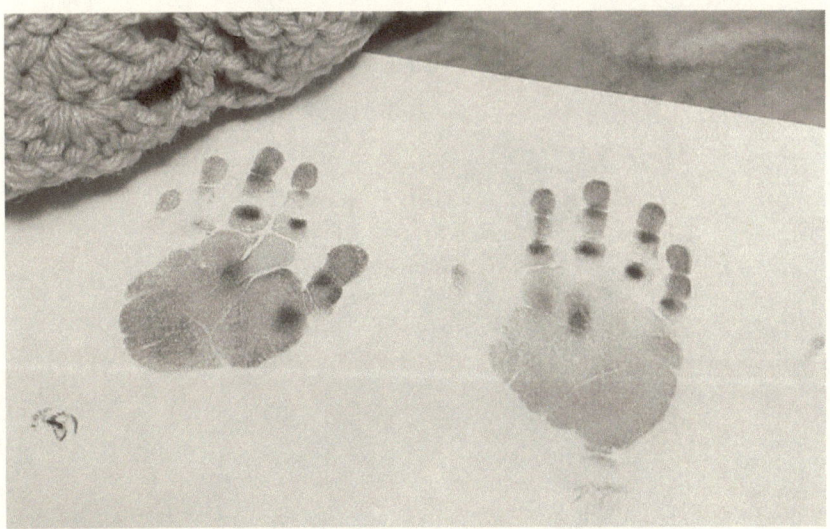

Eli's handprints

and was prepared for labor. I was still in shock that this was it—it was time. I didn't know what to think or feel. There were many emotions. So much to still figure out. But even with all that, our next beautiful baby boy was born the following morning . . . on September 2nd. Seven years to the day that our very first son was due. Our baby Isaac redeemed that day. His birth redeemed September 2nd; the day that should have brought us a son in 2014 brought us one in 2021.

Callen and Isaac won't ever replace Eli. They are blessings all on their own, but they will forever be connected to Eli's story.

And that's the story those high school students heard exactly nine years after I lost Eli. Some of the students in that High School FACS class were, in fact, students in my second-grade class in 2014 when I lost Eli. And I pray that those students received some healing through my sharing of pregnancy loss. I pray they experience healing from God being the gracious and merciful God He is. I pray they learned something from me about sharing my journey of loss and stillbirth.

And I pray for you that after reading my story, you, too, will find some healing and peace. I pray that you will find redemption. Because God is good, and by just having a small, mustard seed–sized amount of faith along this painful path of loss and heartbreak, you can find yourself living a life here on Earth with some peace and patience as you journey toward the best life to come: eternal life with your baby.

Laurel's Story

I *LOVE* AUTUMN. I love the colors of fall leaves, the feeling of crisp air while the sun is shining warm and bright, going to pumpkin patches, you name it—anything involved with fall and I'm there. Autumn also brings along a very busy time of year for me at work. Fall herd work—a physically cumbersome job—is in full swing from late September to December. As a mixed-animal veterinarian, I am busy checking cows for pregnancy, vaccinating and processing calves, figuring out dystocias, and fertility testing bulls.

October of 2017 brought a beautiful change in my life when my husband, Bryce, and I were married after dating for four years. Bryce has been one of the biggest blessings in my life and is a very patient, kindhearted man. Bryce is always supportive of my crazy ideas, loves to try new things and go new places with me, and always takes care of his family before himself. We first found out we were pregnant one month after being married. We were so excited to begin our journey to grow our own family, as well as add to his. Bryce already had an amazing son and daughter, whom we both love very much, from a previous marriage.

With this first pregnancy, my first doctor's appointment was set up at nine weeks. Around four weeks, I developed horrible morning sickness, which lasted all hours of the day and night. The morning of my doctor's appointment, I had a feeling something was off because it was the first time I felt "good and normal" since becoming pregnant. So excited to see our baby, Bryce went with me to my first ultrasound, which revealed a cute, tiny, bean-shaped baby . . . with no heartbeat. The fetal measurements on the ultrasound lined right up with how far I should have been pregnant, indicating a very recent stop of the baby's heartbeat. Damn, the pain and feelings of disappointment of not being able to meet, hold, and take care of our baby in this world!

I was offered a D&C by my doctor, since I was far enough along that I would probably bleed quite a bit when my body released this pregnancy and my baby—which could happen any time. Bryce and I both thought our doctor said "DNC"; we both had never heard of it and had no idea what it was! It turns out a D&C, or Dilatation and Curettage, is performed by dilating the cervix so the uterine lining can be scraped with a curette to remove the nonviable pregnancy. With a physical job that frequently had me working out in the country away from the clinic, I didn't want to risk being caught off guard in the middle of my job having to deal with a messy situation. I was anesthetized later that same day and had a D&C performed.

I came to a realization: I was now in an unspoken "club" that no one ever talked about.

I woke up from the procedure crying; it was the first time I had ever been anesthetized. Three different nurses came up to me before I left the surgical center to tell me they were sorry for what I had just gone through as they all had suffered from miscarriages also. When Bryce brought the car around to pick me up and take me home, I came to a realization: I was now in an unspoken "club" that no one ever talked about or carried on their sleeve so you would know. Even though I felt so alone thinking my body had betrayed me, there were many other women out in the world who had suffered the same loss as me: a miscarriage.

The following day, a Friday, I stayed home from work to recover from my D&C, but I felt absolutely perfect and fine, as if I had never been pregnant. I felt selfish thinking, *Dang, I'll have to start reading that* What to Expect When You're Expecting *book all over again.* Since my morning sickness had been pretty severe, my feelings of normalcy filled me with so much doubt and despair. Did I do the right thing by having a D&C?

What if the baby had still been alive and I didn't know it? Should I have let my body let my pregnancy go naturally so I could know for sure that it was God's plan?

Looking back on it now, I do know the pregnancy was for sure lost. There was no right or wrong answer as to having the D&C performed. I look at ultrasounds frequently for work, and I could see on my ultrasound that the fluid in my uterus was not the nice, dark black, soft tissue/fluid lucency it should have been; it was already getting murky with white floaties in it. The outline of the sweet, bean-shaped baby was also not as sharp and distinct as it should have been. During pregnancy, a baby's heart starts beating around six weeks, and this baby had continued to grow as it should have to get to the nine-week fetal measurement.

I went through so many mixed emotions and felt like I was going through this ordeal all alone! I so desperately wanted to tell my family so they could offer prayers of healing for me, but I felt embarrassed and almost ashamed, as if my body had failed me. I reflect on early miscarriages now as something that God took care of because something was not right. To think about two cells coming together and duplicating at a rapid rate without much room for error is unthinkable! We are all truly gifts from God, and it's a miracle so many babies are born fairly normal with not much more wrong with them.

After our first miscarriage in January 2018, it took Bryce and I four months to get pregnant again. This pregnancy offered the same gift of all-day-and-night morning sickness for me, and though I felt absolutely terrible, I kept reminding myself what a gift it was because the sickness helped me confirm I was still pregnant. As the nine-week mark of this second pregnancy neared, I had so much fear in my heart that my body was also going to let this pregnancy go. It was as if I held my breath until I got past nine weeks and then breathed a huge sigh of relief. Any time I had some relief from my morning sickness and felt "good," I was worried. This blessing of a pregnancy was going flawlessly though; it was normal and healthy for both baby and me. I had an anterior placenta, which means the placenta was located near the front of my abdomen. This blocked me from feeling fetal movements early on, normally around 16 weeks, but I could start to feel this baby move and kick and wiggle around really well at around 24 weeks. This baby was a mover and a groover and loved to boogie when I finally sat down to rest at the end of the day.

On a Thursday evening, when I was 28 weeks along, I thought the baby didn't seem as crazily and actively moving, though he or she was still moving around. With us being crazy busy at work with fall herd work, I just figured I was being too active and needed to rest.

The next day, a Friday, I went out in the afternoon for work to palpate 250 cows for pregnancy. I ran our portable, hydraulic cattle chute for over four hours, my right arm up in the air to run the controls while I pregged cows with my left arm. That evening, when I finally got home and could sit down to rest, I didn't think I felt the baby moving as much, but I just attributed it to being tired and having my body stretched out for half a day while working.

Then the weekend came, and I really felt off. I still felt sick, but the sickness was different, and I didn't think I was feeling the baby move as much. Or at all, for that matter. I was scared to say anything because I didn't want to come off as still worrying all the time, though I did eventually mention it to Bryce. I also didn't want to call and bother anyone at my doctor's office since they were closed. I was already having an ultrasound at my scheduled doctor's visit on Monday, so I would just wait until then to express my concerns.

That Monday morning, Bryce went to my doctor's appointment with me. I first had to chug that nasty little glucose drink to check for gestational diabetes, and then we headed to get our ultrasound. On this day, we saw a new gal who had recently graduated from school and just started working at the Women's Clinic. She was nervous and seemed very slow, fumbling around with the ultrasound probe on my belly and keeping the screen turned toward herself. The young ultrasonographer kept mumbling under her breath, and while she was trying to stay smiley and upbeat, we could tell she was getting frustrated. The first thing I always want to see on a pregnancy ultrasound is a heartbeat, and more importantly, I want to hear that heartbeat. But she still had the screen turned away from us, and after what seemed like an eternity, she got up to excuse herself quickly, saying she'd be right back. We still hadn't heard anything about our baby . . . and we didn't see that ultrasonographer again.

Instead, our doctor quickly came into the room and took over the ultrasound. Bryce and I looked at each other and just knew something was wrong. That's when she turned the ultrasound screen toward us and gently told us our baby did not have a heartbeat. The first words out of my mouth were, "Fuck! I knew it." Our doctor showed us on the ultrasound screen that she thought the umbilical cord was wrapped around our baby's neck at least two times.

My head was reeling. How could this happen again? We were already familiar with a baby with no heartbeat, but *again*? And this far along in my pregnancy? I had just recently breathed a sigh of relief when I made it to twenty-eight weeks with no complications. The third trimester: I was on the downhill slide to being able to meet our sweet baby girl or boy! But now where do we go from here? My emotions were so mixed during this moment: disbelief, pain, frustration, misunderstanding, self-doubt, shock.

After getting some information from my doctor about how to proceed, my husband and I left the clinic and went out to sit in my truck. We needed time to process everything and figure out what we were going to do. It was roughly 9 a.m. on that Monday. Bryce and I were told I would have to be induced to deliver our baby. That was something I absolutely didn't want to do! I dreaded having to deliver a dead baby—but that turned out to be the easiest part of being in the hospital. I just put my head down, bore down, and did it. The absolute hardest part would be leaving my sweet baby behind in the hospital and not being able to take our baby home with us.

I hated everything about this day and all the emotions that came with it. The pain I felt for Bryce was unbearable! In his last relationship, he had lost twins—a boy and a girl, at 24 weeks' gestation—and now he was going through this again. I felt terrible for the new, young ultrasonographer whose day had just been ruined first thing in the morning. I hated that our doctor had to deliver such terrible news to us and then go into her next appointment for a healthy, live baby. I hated that Bryce's older children, Dawson and Hadleigh, would never get to meet their new brother or sister and grow up with him or her. And I was completely devastated that this baby we had longed for and dreamed about would never get to come home with us to be loved unconditionally on this Earth.

Everything about that day was an emotional blur. After lining up someone to watch our older kids at home and contacting some of our family members and work to let them know what was going on, Bryce and I went to the hospital around noon so I could be induced. This was a slow process: a game of sit-and-wait. A prostaglandin pill, misoprostol, was placed near my closed cervix every four hours to induce labor, though I didn't really start feeling menstrual-like cramping until early that evening. The last pill was placed near my cervix around 8 p.m.; that was also the last time my doctor checked on me for the day.

MY AUNT CINDY, who lived in Salina, dropped everything at work to come and sit with Bryce and me for a few hours that afternoon. We were so grateful to have her there as a distraction as she is such a motherly and joyous figure to be around. She had also suffered repeated miscarriages in her and her husband's early days of trying to get pregnant, until they learned that her progesterone levels were not high enough to sustain a pregnancy. Once they figured that out and supplemented her with progesterone, she and her husband were able to have three healthy baby boys.

While Aunt Cindy was there, she also tried to help us name our unborn baby, whom we did not have a name picked out for yet. When she left, Bryce and I finally decided on a couple of names for our baby. My husband and I have never found out the gender of our babies before they've been born. We both think there are no "good surprises" in the world anymore, so we save this intimate moment in the hospital for us to share together. When I was getting induced, we asked the hospital nurses if we could find out the gender of the baby so we could just name him or her. The nurses told us the gender was not written in our chart because they didn't want anyone to accidentally slip up and tell us. While this was a lovely surprise, we still had to pick out a boy's name and a girl's name for our baby. We chose a grandfather's name from both Bryce's family and mine, as well as a grandmother's name from each side of our families.

As the day passed into evening, Bryce watched football on the television while I started to snooze off and on for a while. This whole time, we had a wonderful hospital support staff for whom I will be forever grateful! The nurses were so kind, compassionate, and caring, and we became fast friends. The empathy, compassion, and kindness shown to us by our amazing doctor and nurses will never be forgotten.

AS THE NIGHT PROGRESSED, so did my contractions, which were being monitored on a screen on the wall. From midnight on, these contractions were getting pretty intense, and stacked on top of my pure exhaustion, both physically and mentally, I started to go into almost a panic mode. At 3 A.M., I finally pressed the call button on my bed to ask for an epidural because I could not handle the intense back labor I was having.

A lot of times, though it may be morbid, the way I dealt with tough situations was to try to find some humor in them and crack dumb jokes. The anesthesiologist who waddled in was an older, heavyset man who I could hear mouth-breathing behind me the whole time. I was so relieved when he walked into the room, and I asked him if he was ready for our "hot date," which he was obviously confused by. I continued to crack jokes with him while he prepared me for my epidural to try and get my mind off the pain I was in. He did an excellent job placing my epidural, which started kicking in and relieved me of my pain around 4 a.m. The next hour was the best sleep I've gotten in my life!

At 5 A.M., I woke up to a gush of fluid between my legs as my water finally broke. The nurses called my doctor, who seemed to be there almost immediately. She was so kind and gentle, sitting at the foot of the bed while she helped deliver our baby. The nurses in the room were also soft-spoken and counted down with me while I pushed, helping push on my abdomen to help the baby descend into the birth canal. I could feel my doctor's hands turn the baby inside me as he or she was lying transverse. Bryce stood by my side the whole time, holding my hand and watching as our doctor worked under a blanket to deliver our stillborn baby. When she pulled the baby out from underneath the blanket, Bryce counted as she unwrapped the umbilical cord from our baby's neck three times, not just two like we thought from the ultrasound image. The nurses helped our doctor clamp and cut the baby's umbilical cord. I can still hear my doctor's words as she gently told us we had a baby boy.

A baby boy! Oh, the joy to finally know who was joining our family, but also what pure grief to know we would never get to enjoy this blessing with us here on this Earth! We had longed for this baby for so long and loved him unconditionally even before we met him. It's amazing the love that pours out of you when you get to meet your baby for the first time, though our meeting was also filled with strong feelings of loss, pain, and heart-wrenching grief.

Our baby boy, Forrest Bernard, was absolutely beautiful. He was named after Bryce's maternal grandfather, Forrest, and my paternal grandpa, Mylen Bernard (from my great-grandfather, "Ben"). Our sweet baby had the most perfect, round head with dark hair coming in and a square nose like me. You could see long, dark eyelashes starting to fill in. His poor belly was misshapen from being pulled at the site of the umbilical cord insertion. Ten perfect fingers and ten perfect toes, including the famed "crazy toe" on his right foot, just like his daddy's.

Both my parents, who made a four-hour drive to get there, and Bryce's parents came to see our sweet Forrest that morning. We were so thankful our family could be there to see him and hold him, and their interactions with him are forever imprinted on my heart. Both our fathers were so proud of their new grandson, but I can still see the grief and pain on

Bryce holding sweet Forrest

their faces while they were holding him and looking down on him intently: so proud and yet so sad at the same time. Bryce always said his mother was made to be a mom and grandma on this Earth, and it showed. You could just tell how much our dear Nana loved Forrest. She snuggled him up in a blanket, held him tightly, and rocked him away while beaming at him. I can still see my mother holding Forrest too, smiling down at him and stroking his sweet cheek.

While my mom was visiting us, she took lots of photos on her cell phone of Forrest. My instinctive, protective, mama bear mode instantly kicked in. I didn't want just anyone to have his photo floating around; I wanted to respect his dignity and privacy. I know it may have been a way for her to cope with the situation, but I was really upset with her at the time. That was my baby, who was dead, and she was just shooting all these photos to have him just show up randomly on her phone like any other photo.

About six months later, when I was ready to look at them, I did ask my mom for the photos she took of Forrest. I am now grateful she took them and I have them.

We spent the morning holding and loving on our sweet baby boy. My Aunt Cindy came back to hold our sweet Forrest and brought a beautiful, soft, green blanket for him that she had knitted. We called our priest to

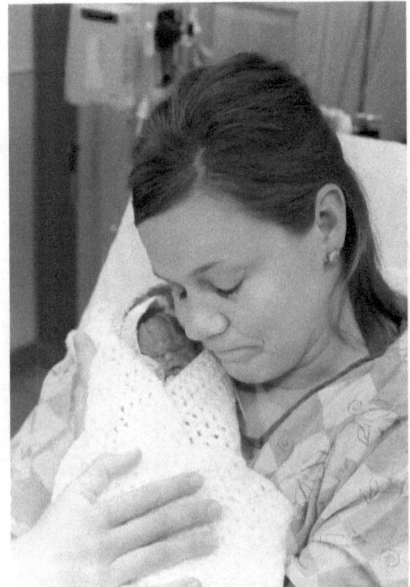 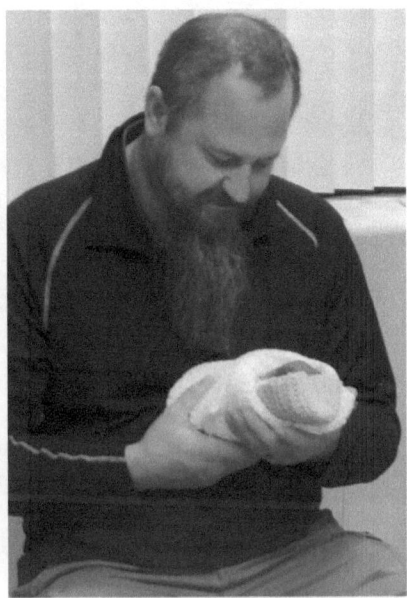

Laurel and Bryce cherishing their short, precious time with Forrest

ask about getting our baby baptized. He told us that God knows the pure intention of the mother's heart, and since Forrest never lived outside of my body, he didn't need to be baptized as he was already a Son of God. This gave us peace of mind, and we already knew that Forrest was up in Heaven looking out for us.

While we had been waiting the previous day for labor to set in, we were able to contact a nonprofit organization called Now I Lay Me Down to Sleep, which connects families with photographers who volunteer their time to take professional black-and-white photos of stillborn or miscarried babies. This is a very kind act that volunteer photographers do at no charge to preserve sweet memories of your precious child. We were emotionally spent and ready to go home when the photographer showed up at our hospital room around noon. After the photos of Forrest were taken, some of him wrapped in a white crocheted blanket from the hospital, we finally decided to go home around 1 p.m.

The morning had been long and short all at the same time and was totally exhausting for us! As time went on, Forrest's skin started drying out since he had already been gone for quite a while. We had three options for taking care of Forrest's body: we could take him home, a funeral home could come pick him up for us, or the hospital would dispose of his body.

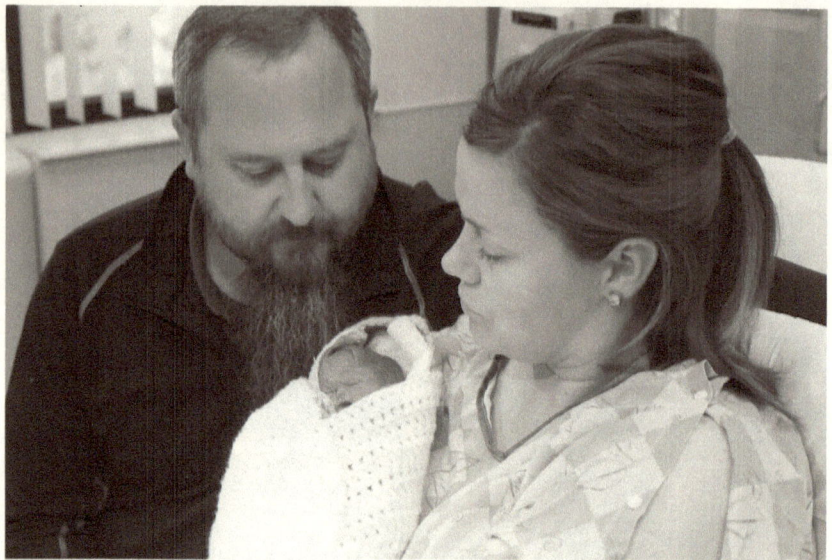

Bryce and Laurel cradling their dear Forrest

We arranged for our hometown funeral home to pick him up later that day and prepare him for a funeral the next day at our cemetery. Leaving Forrest behind in the hospital was, by far, the hardest thing I've ever done in my life. He was our baby—our new, beautiful addition to our family—and he should have been going home with us in the baby carrier.

Bryce and I could not have been more thankful for all the people who helped us out when we lost Forrest. Our funeral director went above and beyond to make us rest assured, after we had to leave our dear Forrest behind in the hospital, that he was handled with the utmost respect and dignity as he was prepared for burial. But we had no idea where to bury our infant son on such short notice. That was when we learned about the dedicated "baby section" in our cemetery: a place where we could bury our baby at no cost when we didn't have cemetery plots for ourselves yet. Our priest and our funeral director took care of everything for the funeral to make it as seamless as possible, and that took so much stress off us during our newly acquired grief.

The next day, a Wednesday right before Thanksgiving, we invited my family and Bryce's family to Forrest's funeral. Some of my siblings packed into a vehicle and made the four-hour trek from Nebraska down to Kansas to be there for us. Bryce and I and his kids, Dawson and Hadleigh, sat in chairs in front of Forrest's tiny casket while our priest gave a graveside service. Our families stood behind us. I could hear someone comment how small the casket was. Bryce's poor nephew passed out during the service because he was going through intense wrestling conditioning for school. I remember the concerned look of a mother on my sister-in-law's face as she put her son in the car so they could take him to the hospital to get IV fluids. Should we have invited other people to be here? Was this too much for everyone else to handle? Again, I started putting others ahead of myself so they wouldn't have to suffer like we were.

Bryce looked totally different that day at the funeral. Bryce's mom would always grab his long beard and joke with him that the new baby would do the same, and he had always promised his mom he would cut it when the new baby came. His mother was starting to get signs of severe dementia and was rapidly changing before our eyes, so we valued all the time we had with her. The night before the funeral, Bryce asked me to braid his long beard so he could cut it off. I sobbed as I braided his beard into two separate braids because I knew how much those things meant to him: his mom, his baby boy, and his beard. We placed one braid of Bryce's beard in the casket with our sweet Forrest and kept the second braid as a memento with Forrest's things.

Thanksgiving was the very next day after we buried our beloved baby. Thanksgiving had always carried a special meaning for Bryce and me because it is the anniversary of when we met at his sister's house. This year, though, happened to be a year we offered to host Thanksgiving at our house. We were still in shock and didn't want to inconvenience anyone, so we just went ahead and hosted. Being busy with the preparations after the funeral was probably a good thing. Bryce and the kids mostly got the house prepared while I just blankly directed them and prepared the food.

Being surrounded by our family and feeling their support that Thanksgiving was such a blessing. I wandered around that day feeling so empty, as if my heart and soul had just been ripped out of me. I also felt like my body betrayed me—I should have still been pregnant. Instead, I was walking around in a big diaper catching my lochia and my breasts were screaming at me in engorgement as my milk came in—a cruel reminder of the baby I had just lost. As painful as that first Thanksgiving was after losing Forrest, I am still thankful our family was able to enjoy Bryce's parents in that moment as they are both now no longer with us here on Earth.

I can still remember how painful my bust was every time someone hugged me, because my milk was coming in. I always thought it was a sick joke that I began lactating because I was making food for a baby, but I had no baby to show for it. Only one nurse in the hospital briefly mentioned using cabbage leaves to help dry up my milk. At the time, I vaguely remember thinking, *Huh.* Not being able to express milk when my breasts were enlarged and hurt so bad was *terrible.* Applying ice packs and taking NSAIDs did help with the pain and inflammation, but cold cabbage leaves gave me the most relief. The pain and betrayal I felt while trying to dry my milk up from being engorged deeply scarred me. I would endure this harsh reminder of losing Forrest after every future baby I delivered as my breasts would become engorged when my milk supply came in.

The following days and weeks were all a blur. I stayed home from work the week after Thanksgiving as my body started healing from delivery, while Bryce returned to work. I mindlessly organized piles of photos into photo albums to keep myself busy. Day after day, I baked an assortment of Christmas cookies so we could give them to our country neighbors. Anything I could do to keep busy and keep my mind off the pain.

When I would get idle and try to rest, tears would take over, and all I could think about was the baby we lost. Our dreams of adding another child to our family were dashed. All the pain from our heart-wrenching loss felt like it would never get better, and I felt like I was going through this whole ordeal alone. I was extremely exhausted and couldn't sleep for months; I kept waking up crying from the gripping loss that was torn out of my body and took my heart with it.

I dreaded having to return to work two weeks after losing Forrest. I really didn't want to go, but I just had to put my head down and do it. I wanted to sit in my living room chair, behind the walls of my house, and hide from the world. I felt so alone in the silence. I didn't want to be confronted by the people who knew about my loss—clients, coworkers, friends, family. The loss was still so acute and raw. I was taken over by immense grief and really didn't know what to do with myself. It was numbing. The feeling of wearing normal jeans to work just two weeks after my loss was crushing. It was as if I'd never had a seven-and-a-half-month pregnant belly on me, and it made me feel shameful and empty. I went through the motions of my job—cattle herd work, dystocias, diagnosing and treating patients, researching difficult cases, performing surgery—without remembering the cases as I went. Any time I became idle at work, just like at home, the grief would unbearably creep back in, so I kept busy.

Just seven short weeks after losing Forrest, my veterinarian business partner and I finalized buying our veterinary practice together. We bought a rural, mixed-animal veterinary clinic—the only animal hospital in two counties—from a senior veterinarian we worked for who was retiring. When we bought our practice, we went from having three veterinarians down to two, so my business partner and I took turns being on call every other night and every other weekend. It was exhausting. I felt like I was on call every single night! As the spring brought on all the new life around us, we were now in our busiest time of year with spring herd work, sick calves, dystocias, and calving issues, on top of still offering excellent care for our small animal patients. I immersed myself in my new ownership role. My business partner and I deep-cleaned our newly acquired business from top to bottom, going through old veterinary supplies and paperwork and making building updates to improve efficiency. Again, keeping busy helped me suppress my grief and helped try to keep my mind off the pain.

In the midst of those seven weeks after losing Forrest, my business partner and I met with a lawyer to form our partnership, as well as an insurance agent to have all the proper legalities set up. Our lawyer had her first baby boy right before I lost Forrest, so she had a playpen/diaper changing station set up in her office for her new infant. When my coworker and I went to her office for meetings to set up our partnership, seeing those baby items for a baby who was just a few months older than mine should have been was a direct punch in the face for me. My heart hurt to be in that room. During that time, I was grieving so hard. I was just going through the motions, signing paperwork as it was explained to me but feeling like I was not really processing the words being spoken to me. I felt like this again when we had to set up protections with our insurance agent; all his insurance jargon went right over my head. I felt so empty and blank, and I spiraled down into depression over the first few months following our loss.

One of Bryce's and my first big "outings" to try and take our minds off things was going to buy new furniture for our living room two months after losing Forrest. The small trip to the furniture store, leisurely driving down the road with the sun shining on our faces, was good for us. Fixing up our 100-year-old limestone house room by room, painting and putting in new flooring as we could afford it, was a good way for us to redirect our grief into something good.

Another way Bryce and I took something ugly and turned it into something good was by doing something in memory of Forrest after we lost him. We considered many different ideas we could do as a tribute to him but ended up deciding against them. We really wanted to plant some trees in the cemetery, since it was our new place we frequented often, but many cemeteries don't want a lot of trees because the root systems may upset the

Bryce and Laurel's children sitting in front of the Marian grotto they dedicated in loving memory of Forrest

headstones. After much contemplating and planning, we recruited a local stone artist, Kirk Robson (Janelle's husband), to build a Marian grotto at our church in April 2021. To say this project was completed beautifully is an understatement! We chose this tribute to Forrest because we believe Christ's mother, Mary, is the mother to all, and we know she is watching out for all the babies and children in Heaven until their parents are reunited with them once again. Now when we come to church and see that Marian grotto in the courtyard, it's like getting a warm hug from our sweet boy, who is looking out for us and is under Mother Mary's loving care until we can be reunited with him in Heaven one day.

BRYCE AND I GREW STRONGER in our relationship together because we shared this loss and leaned on each other to get by. We spent many nights in the kitchen after work talking about our sweet baby boy and what we thought he would be like. I never felt bad talking or crying about Forrest with Bryce and sharing my feelings of loss and hurt, hope and faith. Bryce did ask me a few times in the first couple of years if I thought I needed to see a counselor, but I was stubborn and refused, hoping time would heal my wounds. Many times, these "mini sessions" in the kitchen with Bryce slowly helped my heart to heal because I could get those heavy feelings off my chest.

Everything blurred together for *at least* the first year after our loss. The only way I later recognized I had depression was that I started to feel like I was lifting out of a fog over one year later. At the time, I had no idea I was depressed. I just knew I didn't feel like myself and I was just not happy. I also just lost faith, which had been such an integral part of my life—it seemed to just vanish overnight, out of my control. I could not pray, sing in church, reference anything holy, give thanks for my blessings, nothing. I was not mad at God and didn't blame Him or anyone else, but I was completely blank and struggled with the words to say to Him.

I honestly didn't know if I'd ever feel "normal" again, and I was so sad about losing my baby boy. Pre-loss, I was always the person up for a good time; I was spirited and joyous, always joking around, and genuinely loved people and life. I didn't recognize this new person post-loss, and I grieved the person I used to be. I know I am now *harder* than I used to be; simple things that used to bring me joy are now just things to me.

A part of my "new" self feels like I always have my ear on the ground, listening for that next woman who lost her baby so I may find a way to reach out to her to offer my support. I *never* want another person to go through the loss of a baby or child like we have, and I would rather take on all that pain so another person does not have to endure it. A Facebook group of bereaved parents I was added to after our loss helped me get through some of my toughest and darkest days. Being able to have other parents' kind words and support meant the world to me. Through that group, I was also able to offer my condolences to other parents going through some of the same losses, and it was nice to know I was not alone even on the darkest of days.

Though the loss of my "old self" is still hard, I've learned to continue looking for joy in everything—even the hardest of situations—and thank the Lord for all His blessings. Some of our biggest blessings after losing our sweet Forrest were having three beautiful babies added to our family: a daughter, Oaklynn; a daughter, Karter; and a son, Ledger. Our very first stop on our way home with all three babies was to visit their big brother, Forrest, in the cemetery. While these beautiful additions to our family are

New siblings visiting big brother, Forrest, on their way home from the hospital

such a blessing and bring us so much joy, we still grieve the loss of our sweet Forrest as he can *never* be replaced. So much beauty and so much sorrow.

Before these three blessings were added to our family, we had another heartbreaking loss with an early miscarriage in June 2019, seven months after delivering Forrest still. A hard journey of unexplained infertility was very tough and trying for Bryce and me and added worry, fear, and stress into our relationship, on top of all the other emotions I was struggling with after losing Forrest. Even after delivering healthy babies, I would worry nonstop about things outside of my control, such as sudden infant death syndrome in the first year of life. To ease my worry, help calm my fears, and give me peace of mind, I used an Owlet oxygen and respiration tracker on the foot of all three of my babies at night while they were sleeping. I also had to start working on my faith again, making an effort to put more of my trust back in the Lord, to "let go and let God."

As with Forrest, we did not find out the gender of our babies during our other pregnancies either. When our first daughter, Oaklynn, was born via emergency cesarean section, I was so happy, relieved, and elated when they pulled that baby out of my belly. I started crying the moment I heard the baby cry because I knew he or she was still alive and was safe. But when they showed us the baby from behind the surgery curtain, even through the immense joy I was feeling, I felt a brief pang of disappointment that we'd had a girl. In that brief second, I longed for a boy, hoping to fill the void in our hearts from our sweet Forrest not being in our family. I was so ashamed to feel that way as our first baby girl was the best gift we could have ever been given, and God definitely knows what He's doing when He gives us our blessings. Our children have been such a blessing for our family, and it's such a privilege that God entrusted them to us to take care of them here on this Earth and for me to be their momma.

Even though seven years have now passed, I still have my good days and my bad days. The bad days always seem to come out of nowhere and are really tough. Then, when they seem to dissipate a little, I realize a major anniversary like Forrest's due date or the anniversary of his delivery is coming up. It's like my body just knows and my hormones fluctuate without my mind actually thinking about it. Those are the days I really know I cannot do this on my own and just have to rely on God to carry me through.

Often, when I'm having a sad day, something will show up out of nowhere and surprise me—most definitely a sign from God to take heart and know He is near. For me, a reminder of Forrest may be seeing a cardinal fly across the road in front of my truck. Other days it's a rainbow cast across my living room floor. I teach my children that Jesus is always present in our hearts. One day when I was missing my sweet Forrest, Oaklynn was snuggling next to me on the couch, and out of nowhere she said, "Forrest is in my heart." It meant the world to me that she said that, lifting me up in that moment, and it's those little things that give me hope and help me get by until I can be reunited with my baby again someday. Can you just imagine, getting to Heaven and hearing a voice you don't know say, "Mommy!"? That alone gives me strength and hope.

In 2024, Forrest presented to me as a "guardian angel" specifically for my new niece, Lydia. During my sister's pregnancy with Lydia, she had been seeing specialists because the doctors suspected their baby did not have a functioning kidney. All the uncertainty about this sweet baby girl's kidneys working or not and whether her health in general would be good was so unnerving. We prayed so hard for this baby girl so she would not have all the health complications their doctors were concerned about. As Lydia's due date grew near, and my sister began to have complications with the pregnancy, a great wave of peace and reassurance washed over me when Lydia was delivered early on Forrest's due date, February 15th. This was a sign to all of our family that Lydia's complicated health issues with her kidneys would be okay as Forrest would watch over her and guide her through. Today Lydia is a beautiful, happy-go-lucky, thriving toddler with one normally functioning kidney who will continue to be monitored throughout her life. Lydia also happens to be my nephew, Jameson's, little sister. God always seems to work in mysterious ways, and God is good!

My biggest fear is that my sweet Forrest will be forgotten, even though he lives on forever in our hearts. When I reached out to my friend Kelvi on Karaline's fifth birthday, I just wanted to let her know her sweet daughter was not forgotten. I had *sobbed* in the truck on our way out of the lawyer's office, which was next door to Kelvi's flower shop at the time, when my business partner told me of their loss just three short weeks after ours.

And when an unexpected limestone rock with a heart on it showed up on the mound of dirt that was Forrest's grave, I remember being so protective and getting mad that someone had put it there. But after reading a letter that accompanied the beautifully carved rock, we found out it was a gift from Janelle and her husband, Kirk. We learned of them wanting to spread joy through the heartbreak they suffered from the loss of their baby boy, Eli. I thought Janelle and Kirk were so strong and resilient, letting Eli's legacy live on through his parents' good work. I am now reminded of Janelle's sweet boy, Eli, every time I look at the "Joy" rock which sits on the piano in our living room. I pray that you, too, will find a support system like these two women have been for me—to help guide you through some of your toughest days, to share about your good days, and to just lend a listening ear when you need it.

The fierce love you have for the baby you lost will never change—but you may learn to direct that love into a positive outlet so the memory of your sweet baby may live on.

Just as the fall will turn into winter and winter into spring, you will find the only thing that doesn't change is change. This will turn out to be a good thing for you, and you will grow with it. It may take every ounce of your being to be able to forge on and feel like you can begin to live again, but you can do it—you *will* do it! The deep, dark hole of loss, grief, and depression will get better—you *will* get through it. You may feel like you're finally moving forward and are then pushed a few steps back, finding yourself changing once again. The fierce love you have for the baby you lost will never change—but you may learn to direct that love into a positive outlet so the memory of your sweet baby may live on and something, or someone, may benefit from it. You may not be the same version of yourself that you used to be, and that's okay; you will continue to be shaped into something new and different from the change that is ever-evolving.

I love you, sweet momma, and I am here for you—you can *do* this. And please know your sweet baby will *never* be forgotten.

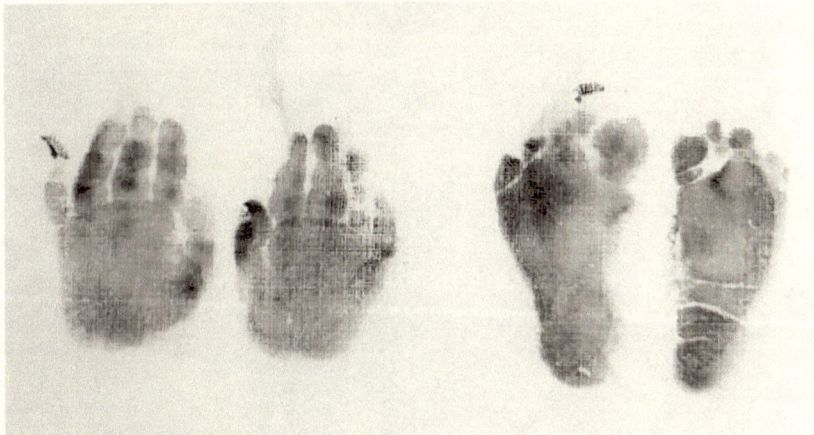

Forrest's handprints and footprints

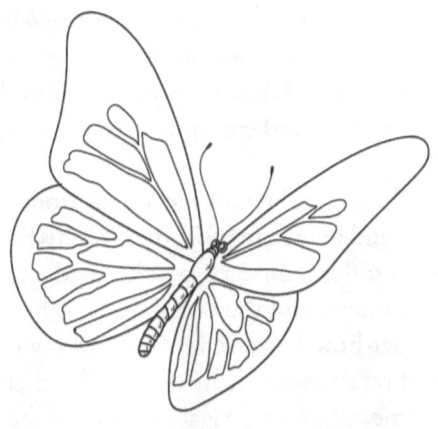

Kelvi's Story

BEFORE I GET INTO MY STORY, I want to start by telling you how hard it was for me to put it out there. But not for the reasons you might think. No, it wasn't because I couldn't find the right words, or dig into old emotions that I had stuffed deep down inside, or admit that I suffered through things like depression and shame. In fact, it was something else. I felt like my loss wasn't significant enough to be told.

Love, feelings, and emotions aren't discredited
by gestational time limits.

Early in the book planning phase, I told my coauthors that we needed to put my story last. "Not many people will want to read about a miscarriage at only 16 weeks along," I told them. "Some people don't even consider it a baby at that point, let alone acknowledge a loss like that as a big deal." As I started to hit the gas pedal down the hill of self-doubt, I almost had myself convinced to pull my part completely. "You didn't carry your baby as long as your coauthors did," I'd tell myself. "Not many people care." But then

I hit the brakes on the downhill slide of doubt and negativity. *You didn't write this for the people who don't care,* I reminded myself. *You wrote it for the ones who went through the same thing you did and feel alone.* My loss may not be as heavy as my coauthors'. I didn't carry my baby in the womb as long as they did. But love, feelings, and emotions aren't discredited by gestational time limits.

Shortly after my loss, I was literally met on my front door by two remarkable women: Janelle and Laurel, my coauthors of this book. As I was the last of the three of us to suffer a miscarriage, they had, unfortunately, already begun their grief journeys, and they were ready to hold my hand through mine. I often wonder how I would've managed my miscarriage without their guidance and reassurance. I am so thankful that they opened their hearts and arms to me, all while navigating losses of their own.

In the next several pages, I share the loss of my daughter Karaline. I share it not because I feel like I overcame some insurmountable loss. I share it because I've learned that there are millions of women who have experienced a miscarriage below a certain threshold of gestation who are suffering and feel alone. They don't have a Laurel or a Janelle to show up at their front door, to hold their hand and say, "I understand, and you're going to get through this." Gestational limits are not timelines for grief, nor do they dictate your feelings. I wrote this for the women who need to hear these same words that are often shared with me: You are not alone, and your loss and your feelings matter.

December 8, 2018

Life is always so busy. Being the owner of the only flower and gift shop in a bustling small town seems like the ultimate dream. But it was December 8, 2018, and on days like today, it is everything but. Christmas Open House can be our busiest weekend of the year in sales, and in an effort to entice more foot traffic through the shop, I offered free lunch in the back. Combine that with "the more you buy, the more you save" discounts, free gift wrapping, and Christmas just a few weeks away, you manage to pull off quite the marketing ploy. The shop was buzzing with activity. Christmas greens had arrived, the cooler needed to be refreshed, inventory was constantly needing to be restocked, and customers needed more attention than ever to find the personalized, "just right" gift or arrangement.

By the end of the day, I was exhausted. I finished washing out the last five-gallon bucket and lifted several clean ones full of water and flowers back into place on the shelves of the floral cooler. Being almost sixteen weeks pregnant, I was ready to head home and get some much-needed rest. I had spent several long days preparing for this event, and I told myself to take it easier at the shop, but asking for additional help from my staff made me feel uncomfortable. As the business owner, I tried to lead by example. I could certainly wash buckets, clean coolers, and stack tables and chairs just like everyone else. The reality, however, was that my body was tired, and it needed a slower pace. Any of my staff would lend a helping hand when necessary, and all I had to do was ask. But for some reason, asking for help was hard to do and made me feel like I was being a burden to others.

I finished up at the shop and finally headed home for the day. I pulled up to our simple, ranch-style home, a few blocks away, to be greeted by my three daughters and husband outside. Kinly, my oldest, was nine, Kari was seven, and Kacy was four. My husband, Karlton, was being his usual self and playing with the girls outside as the devoted father he is. When it comes to a husband and father, I hit the jackpot. Karlton and I had been married for ten years, and while we had our ups and downs, he was my rock. I gave my usual greeting and, exhausted, quickly went inside to find the restroom. After sitting down, I gasped at what was there—a large gathering of blood. I finished in the restroom and went to find Karlton. I told him my concern, but since it had seemed to stop, I decided it best just to lie down and rest from the terribly busy day on my feet and heavy lifting. There had been some spotting with this pregnancy since about eight weeks along, but nothing had been this heavy. My previous three pregnancies with the girls were all healthy and full-term with no complications. I reassured myself that some much-needed rest and lying down would be just what my body and this baby needed to recuperate.

Three days later, on Tuesday, December, 11, I woke up to another large pool of blood. Alarmed at the size of the issue, I decided to call my OB-GYN office. I spoke with the nurse, who was very sweet and reassuring. She said she would speak with Dr. Parriott, my doctor, and give me a call back. A few short moments later, she called. My doctor thought everything would be all right, especially since I was feeling okay and not experiencing any contractions, but if I wanted some reassurance, I could come over to the clinic for an ultrasound. However, since this ultrasound was between my routine ultrasounds and insurance considered it unnecessary, we would have to pay for it—roughly $1,000—out of pocket. Karlton and I discussed our options and ultimately decided that this was worth paying for. I had to put my mind at ease that this baby was okay. I called the shop to let my staff know that I wouldn't be there today, feeling like I was burdening them by asking them to cover for me. *Why do you feel so guilty about prioritizing your health and your baby?* I thought to myself. Fourth quarter was our busiest season at the shop, and while it ran efficiently without me, I still felt guilty and selfish that I was taking the day off for myself and this baby.

A few hours later, I was looking at my beautiful, perfect baby on the screen of the ultrasound. Karlton and I were unsure yet if it was a boy or a girl, but deep down, I hoped for a boy. I struggled to see if I could make out any clues, but the baby was so active that he or she was doing somersaults in my tummy. Little fists were pumping away, and it was too hard to identify any gender-revealing parts. The ultrasound tech printed off several pictures and gave us a DVD of the live action of our beautiful baby. We left the facility to go back to meet with Dr. Parriott, joking that this is what $1,000 worth of ultrasound pictures looked like. Little did I know, it was the best $1,000 I'd ever spent.

Inside an exam room, Dr. Parriott made his usual boisterous appearance. "How's my favorite couple?" he'd tease. Dr. Parriott had been my OB-GYN since I was a teenager. He was the epitome of an OB-GYN. He had an extremely funny sense of humor, but he always kept it professional. Karlton and I had the utmost respect for him over the years as he had been absolutely fabulous delivering the three girls. And his job wasn't always easy: our last delivery was anything but smooth. Kacy had ended up being stuck with shoulder dystocia, and after a very stressful delivery, Dr. Parriott told us that if we were to have any more children, they would all be delivered via cesarean section. To this day, we credit his experience and knowledge to saving her from trauma and any physical disabilities. Our first daughter, Kinly, was a whopping 9 lb. 6 oz. when she was born, and subsequently, Kari and Kacy were induced a week early due to size. I often joke that the first question to ask on a first date is "How much did you weigh when you were born?" because Karlton's 9 lb. 11 oz. birth weight seemed to be carrying over.

Dr. Parriott looked over the ultrasound and my chart and informed us that there was a small placental abruption occurring, and that is what had been causing the bleeding. He went on to explain that due to its small size, he was confident that it would fix itself. He said, "Generally, 99 out of 100 of these fix themselves, and there is conflicting information about bed rest at this point." He advised not overdoing it but rather trying to take it easy and continuing with a normal routine. We left the office and drove home feeling very relieved and happy.

The next morning, Wednesday, December 12, I awoke to contractions. I lay in bed for a while, thinking they would surely subside, but they continued to worsen. I called one of my lifelong friends who was a local doctor here in my hometown of Ellsworth. She sensed something off in my voice as I was short of breath while talking with her. She advised getting to either my OB-GYN's office, the ER in town, or the ER in the neighboring city of Salina, which was about 35 minutes away. Karlton got the girls to school and daycare and returned home, his concerns also mounting. He called my shop manager to tell her that I was not feeling well and wouldn't be coming into the shop again today. Once again, a sense of guilt took over me. I felt like I was being a burden to my staff by asking them to cover yet another busy day at the shop without me.

We loaded into the car and began the 35-minute drive to Salina. The car couldn't go fast enough. About halfway there, my contractions grew into excruciating physical pain, and the terror of losing my baby escalated. At this point in the drive, Karlton's concern worsened. He kept trying to reassure me, "We're almost there, sweetheart." All I remember saying is, "HURRY! HURRY!" I'm not sure what I expected Salina Regional ER to do for me, but *someone* had to help me and save this baby. Finally, we rounded the last turn and entered the homestretch into Salina. I held on to the overhead grab handle as tightly as I could, but even more than that, I held to the hope that this would all turn out all right.

We finally reached Salina. As the physical pain continued to increase, the distance to the hospital was reduced. Only a few more blocks to go. If I can manage this pain for just a little bit longer, relief will be here soon. Then we got stopped by a red light at a left turn onto Santa Fe Avenue. The hospital was within reach. I could see it. Just three short blocks away. Karlton was anxious to get there, but he could not turn us into oncoming traffic coming down Crawford Street. And then it all stopped, right there at that traffic light. The contractions and the pain were gone.

But as the physical pain subsided, a new and unwelcome feeling of fear grew. Fear that perhaps the laboring contractions had ceased because it was over, because my body had miscarried this pregnancy.

About as quickly as I shoved that thought aside, we turned onto Santa Fe Avenue. The hospital was within reach, and so was the hope that perhaps it had just been contractions and the baby was all right. Somewhere along the drive to the hospital, Karlton had called to let them know that we were on our way and that his wife was possibly in labor. Upon arrival at the ER bay, we were met outside by someone with a wheelchair. I was helped off of my seat and into the chair, but I couldn't help but notice the amount of blood on the seat of the car.

Once I was inside the ER waiting room, they wheeled me over to a check-in desk. *Ridiculous,* I thought to myself. *Get me to a room already.* I recall resting my head on my fist, which I had balled, and my arm sitting at a 90-degree angle with my elbow on the armrest. The check-in clerk was polite, but I was so angry at her that we even had to check in to begin with. If the hastiness of my voice didn't send the message, I was hoping that my body language would. *Just get me to a room already,* I kept thinking.

After what seemed like an eternity of scanning insurance cards and IDs, I was wheeled into a room and met with a nurse, who also called in two labor and delivery nurses. The nurse suggested that I try to stand up. Once I did, I was helped to the restroom. I felt so weak from the waist down. Karlton never left my side. He followed us into the bathroom, where my sweet baby exited my body.

I remember saying something like, "Oh, no!" or "Oh, God!" The nurses tried to distract me and helped me over to the bed. My instinct knew what had just been delivered, but my mind wouldn't let me believe it. Surely there was a chance I had just lost a lot of blood and clots. A chance my baby was still alive and inside of me. From my resting place on the bed, I could see straight into the bathroom. And that's when I saw Karlton. I will never forget the look on his face. It's a look that is burned into my memory forever. I looked to my right, and we made eye contact. My eyes were filled with tears, and I silently pleaded for an answer. He stood over a rolling table, one arm crossed at his midsection, and the other bent at the elbow, his hand resting against his jaw. He looked at me with a sad, desperate, defeated look and simply nodded. As two nurses hovered over a small table, they picked apart the mess that would reveal my baby. Heartbreak and sorrow overtook me, and so did the harsh realization of what just happened. My baby was gone.

A few minutes later, one of the nurses announced it was a girl. Shock and disbelief had overcome me. The reality of losing my baby was just not something I was willing to accept. I also recall a selfish, yucky feeling of disappointment that it was another girl. Deep down, I had wanted a boy. We already had three girls, and I so desperately wanted a boy. Karlton was the only boy with five sisters, and the future of the Place name rested on him. At the same time, I felt a huge pang of sadness because I wouldn't have another sweet Place girl to bring home. Karlton is the most amazing dad a girl could ever ask to be married to, and any child would be so lucky to have him as a father. Many people have given him a hard time over the years because he is so protective of our three girls. That instinct was on full display as he watched those nurses carefully to make sure they handled his fourth girl with respect and care.

On my ER bed, I sat alone and defeated. A nurse brought a sonogram machine over to me, and as she rolled the cold stick over my abdomen, I craned my neck to look at the screen. "What are you looking for?" I asked her. I was still holding out hope, even at this point, that somehow, this was all wrong. Perhaps that wasn't my baby in the bathroom, and she was still inside of me. The nurse informed me that she was looking for any remaining tissue that could cause me further bleeding or other problems. She mustn't have found much as she quickly put the machine away and didn't say anything. *Why isn't she saying anything?* I thought to myself. *Please just say something, anything, to make me feel better. Or if nothing else, please just say, "I'm sorry."* Her silence made me feel isolated and alone.

After several minutes of this, Karlton came to sit next to me. I scanned the room, and my eyes met a small purple box sitting on the counter across from my bed. I will never forget what came next. A nurse exiting the room asked us, "Do you want me to dispose of it?"

"No!" I replied with a sharp, unrelenting tone. "We'll take *her* home, thank you."

I could not believe the question she had just asked me. Dispose of *it*? *It*? Was this not a baby inside this box? What did she mean by dispose? Throw away? More questions began circling in my head. Why would this *baby* not be treated like a *person*? Am I being asked this because I'm only in my second trimester and not the third?

As my anger flared, Karlton tried his best to calm me down. "Do you want to see her?" he asked. I nodded, too upset to speak. He brought the box over to me and laid it on my lap. I opened it up to see our baby. There *she* was. *She* was the most beautiful thing to me. *She* was small enough to fit in the palm of my hand but had developed the most beautiful, delicate features, with a nose just like her sister's. They had done an amazing job of cleaning her up. Whether they did this on purpose or not, they had placed her tiny hand over her heart. I felt like this was her message of telling me, 'I love you, Mom.'

"What should we name her?" I asked Karlton.

"I was thinking Karaline," he replied. It felt like the perfect fit, and I nodded in agreement. My heart wasn't ready for me to say her name. He took the box back over to the counter, and the nurse informed us we couldn't leave just yet. Dr. Parriott was on his way down to see us. Later, I had learned that one of the labor and delivery nurses had informed Dr. Parriott that I had just miscarried in an ER room, and he told her to not let me leave until he was able to come see me.

A short while later, a very somber Dr. Parriott entered the room and took a seat next to me. "Kelvi, I am so sorry," he said. "When I saw you in my office yesterday, I was certain it was going to fix itself." I sobbed and looked up to see a tear leave his eye. *Wow,* I thought to myself. *I am not just a number to him. What a beautiful act of kindness for him to take the time to not only come and console us but also want to see Karaline as well.* He told us she was beautiful, said something to the nurses, and left.

After going through the discharge papers about what to watch out for physically, we were told we could go home. To this day, I reflect on this moment. I am saddened and disappointed that while we were provided with information about my physical well-being, we were given nothing that would help me emotionally. Not one trifold pamphlet or list of resources that would help equip me for the emotional journey I was about to take. Nothing that could help me unravel and comprehend what had just happened. And nothing to let me know that I was not alone in what I had just experienced.

Karlton and I exited the room together, side by side, in what was the most humiliating moment of my 33 years of life. Karlton, carrying the purple box that held my sweet Karaline, walked down the hall next to me as we started our trip home. We were the unfortunate parents leaving the hospital with our baby in a box, not a car seat. I remember people looking at us in the ER lobby and just feeling utter defeat. *What a failure of a woman you are,* I thought to myself. *You just failed not only this baby but also your husband and three girls at home who thought they were going to have another sibling.* This extreme shame would follow me hard for a few years.

THE FOLLOWING DAYS all seemed to flow together. And so did the emotions. The first obstacle to overcome was figuring out what we were supposed to do with her when we got home. In our home state of Kansas, the gestation limit for a death certificate to be issued is twenty weeks. Because she was a little over sixteen weeks along, we had no guidance on a burial or whether we should have a funeral or not. We both knew for sure that we wanted to bury her properly, but where?

Karlton went down to our local funeral home. They were very sympathetic and willing to do whatever we needed. We contemplated burying her in our backyard, at my grandmother's farm, or in our local cemetery. After weighing the pros and cons, we decided to place her next to Karlton's father, George, at our local cemetery just a few blocks away. Karlton went to the local hardware store and bought a fireproof/waterproof safe, and that is what we placed her and her little purple box in. She was buried the very next day after she was delivered.

I don't remember a lot from that day, but here is what I remember most. I did not want to be there. Our pastor performed a brief committal. We had invited a few very close friends and family members. The weather was awful. The Kansas wind decided to show her true colors and blow about 40 miles per hour. I remember standing there and being so angry. I was angry that I even had to stand there at all. I couldn't wait for it to be over. As soon as our pastor had finished speaking, I started walking to our car by myself. It was parked in one of the alley drives of the cemetery with a straight-shot view of Karaline's resting place. I got in the car and looked over to witness another heart-wrenching scene: Karlton was shoveling dirt on top of her. He had taken it upon himself to bury her. I knew he would want to do this, but I couldn't help but think, *He should be walking her down the aisle to her wedding one day, not putting dirt on top of her.*

Sitting in the car alone, my attention was turned to another problem. I was not physically healing from the miscarriage, and instead, I was bleeding heavily. The ER nurses had tried their best the day before to assure me that I was physically okay. Holding on to the hope that they were right, we decided against going to the hospital and went home.

The next morning, I awoke to even more blood. After a few phone calls to Dr. Parriott's nurse, she was concerned I needed a D&C procedure due to leftover tissue in my uterus. With it being a Friday, we had to load up quickly and get over to the surgical hospital before it closed at noon. The nurse informed me on the phone that Dr. Parriott was off that day, so the procedure would be done by someone else. I was so disheartened. He had been there with me through all of this, and I trusted him. Nevertheless, we drove back over to Salina and checked into the surgical hospital, which was right across the street from the hospital where I had delivered Karaline just at two days prior. Arriving at the surgical hospital gave me a sense of relief that feeling better physically was now a possibility, but seeing the ER bay across the street brought back an immediate feeling of pain and sadness, along with a reminder that I was without my baby inside of me.

After check-in, I was assigned to one of those not-so-private "rooms" partitioned off with sheets hanging from the ceiling. Being alone with

Karlton was hard because I was carrying such deep emotions: guilt, shame, and, quite simply, regret for letting him down. He stood next to my bed and continually reassured me that this wasn't my fault and that there was nothing we could have done differently. He was so supportive and attentive to me.

After about 30 minutes of waiting, due to the lack of actual walls, I was able to recognize a very characteristic voice a few feet away. It was Dr. Parriott. He had come in on his day off to do my procedure. I can't put into words what his compassion still means to me, but I am so very grateful. It was now my turn for the D&C procedure. One of the nurses came in to our "room" and warned us that when I came out of the procedure, emotions might take over and I could experience some heartache. *That's odd,* I thought to myself. *How can I feel any worse?* Karlton kissed me goodbye on the head, and they wheeled me back to the surgery room and gave me anesthesia. I later learned from one of the nurses that while going under the anesthesia, I told them, "Don't tell Karlton how much shopping I've been doing."

That was the last funny thing I said for a while because they weren't lying when they said I'd feel emotional when I came to. I awoke after the procedure a complete sobbing mess. I cried, and I cried *hard*. My emotions were absolutely out of control. This was the first time in my life that I had experienced true, raw emotions spilling out from me that I could not rein in. Thankfully, I had the sweetest nurse, who I went to church with, there by my side. I was so glad to awaken to a familiar face rather than a stranger. She sat next to my bed and just hugged me and let me cry into her shoulder.

After a few hours in recovery, I was sent home. All of the physical pain and ailments were seemingly behind me. The emotional journey, however, had only just begun.

February 1, 2024—Approximately 5 years later

I readjusted the plates and napkins and moved the chips and queso around for what seemed like the twelfth time, trying to calm my nerves. I was having two ladies over for dinner, hoping they liked Mexican food and praying that the question I was about to ask them wouldn't make them think I was crazy. Creating a positive table of friends was something my psychologist had challenged me to do at my last mental health therapy session a few weeks prior. I took the assignment quite literally at first by asking Janelle and Laurel over to eat around my dining room table. Figuratively, however,

I was about to ask them to embark on a journey that would grow our table much bigger than I could ever have imagined.

Janelle arrived first, and we caught up on life and kids. Little did she know how much I had looked up to her over the last decade. Losing a baby at 38 weeks was something that seemed unimaginable to get over, yet she continued to live life for a bigger calling, both to God and to other women going through loss, myself included. Janelle was there right after I lost Karaline, dropping off a "Joy" rock on my porch with a heartfelt note, and she was there through some of the roughest patches of my grief journey. I didn't do a great job of letting my emotions come out in the beginning, like she did. Instead, I shoved them deep down to be almost inaccessible. Years after my loss, the perfect storm of stress and reminders of Karaline erupted all at once, and I found myself hitting the proverbial gas pedal down a deep, dark road of grief and depression. I was so thankful for the times she would answer my phone call when I thought I just couldn't get past a certain feeling or emotion, or the time she dropped off a Bible study series at just the right time.

Laurel arrived a few minutes later, dressed in scrubs but glowing. She was about six months pregnant, and while having two little ones at home and owning her veterinarian clinic didn't leave her much free time, I could tell her curiosity had gotten the best of her as to why I'd asked her and Janelle over for dinner. Laurel, too, was such a blessing to me during my loss journey. Having lost her baby just a month prior to me losing Karaline, she showed enormous strength in being at my front door, both right after and on several anniversary dates of Karaline's birthday. In fact, she was just at my front door two months prior to that night with a beautiful gift to remember our babies on that five-year milestone.

As the three of us began eating our fajitas, the small talk had started to run its course, and my two friends were now asking what this "crazy idea" was that had brought us all together. "I'm going to throw something at you two, and if you want to just finish dinner and leave, I understand," I said. Laurel wondered what kind of fundraiser I wanted to put on, or if I was going to reopen my flower shop that I had sold shortly after my miscarriage. And Janelle just continued to stay quiet. "No, it's not a fundraiser or a business," I teased. "That would be easier." I couldn't hold the suspense any longer, so finally, I blurted out, "We should write a book!"

Laurel leaned back in her chair and immediately responded with, "Whoa! I'm no writer. And you're right, a fundraiser would've been easier."

I couldn't help but turn my attention to Janelle, who was silent and appeared deep in thought. "What do you think, Janelle?" I asked her. "Or do you just think I'm crazy?"

Janelle's demeanor turned from stoic to amazed. "You two are never going to believe what was in my devotional last night," she said.

"What?" I asked.

She continued, "If God calls you to write, you should write."

It was one of those "only God" moments for all three of us. A moment when the hair on your arms stands up. A moment when you know that something just feels right. A moment of validation. Shortly before the two of them arrived, I was so nervous that I went into my bedroom, got down on my hands and knees, and asked God to be in our conversation that night and to lead and guide us in our fellowship. And that is exactly what He did for the next year and a half.

Writing this book was something that none of the three of us had any time for. It was hard. It was emotional. It was labor-intensive. But for me, it was the path to healing that I needed. Within the companionship of my coauthors, I was finally able to speak my silence about the grief, shame, and guilt that I was carrying for so long. Their advice during tough times of navigating through emotions that I had stuffed away for five years was a gift I can never repay them for.

But most of all, I found that there is a community of women just like Janelle and Laurel, who have been through unimaginable loss, who choose to live for more and honor their babies. Women who choose to see the joy in the grief. To live for God's glory and their families. To put themselves aside and show up for others. Women who will meet you at the front door of your grief, invite you to sit at a table where you don't feel alone, walk alongside you when the days seem dark, and provide you with the tools and the love to get you through your journey. I hope that in the following pages, you can use the tools we've found useful ourselves to begin your healing journey. To step out of the silence. To live through the grief and find joy again.

Kelvi's daughters visiting Karaline's gravesite

Part 2

SURVIVAL TOOLS

We want to start this section of the book by again saying, "We're sorry." We are so very sorry you find yourself here in the hardness, quiet, and oftentimes bitterness of losing a baby. We are absolutely heartbroken that you are walking this road of grief. We don't know your exact situation. We don't know what makes your loss specific and personal to you. But we do know your loss matters. We know your loss is hard. We know you may find yourself needing a community of support from people who know grief. Whether the journey you find yourself on is for your own personal walk or that of a family member or dear friend, we are very truly sorry you are here.

Our hope is for you to find support and community within these pages. We want to offer you survival insight, as well as quotes, journal entries, and personal experiences that may help you face some hard moments. We hope to give you insight on how to face difficult people and hard experiences. We want to encourage you to keep living with yourself even when you feel like you can't. This section is designed to offer you or someone you care about survival strategies. We want to offer opportunities for support that all three of us considered key components to our individual journeys of surviving the trauma of fetal demise. We encourage you to take the parts that resonate within your soul—the parts that speak to your healing, the parts that make you say, "Me too" or "I totally understand that," or the parts that have you thinking, "I think that might be what I need"—we encourage you to take those opportunities and strategies and make them your own.

If you find yourself needing to survive a rude comment or person, an unwanted feeling, or a string of doubt and despair, this section offers tips. If you find yourself questioning "how" or "why" or even "now what," we offer this section to you as a point of hope. It's a place to go when you can't go anywhere else; it's a place of support. It's a place where you can survive. We'll say it now and again through your reading: We want to meet you at your front door and be here with you throughout your journey.

Surviving the Right After—
Our Letter to You

To the Woman Who Is Surviving the Right After,

You can do this! You can . . . do this! We know your intense level of pain seems unbearable right now. It feels as if your whole world is broken and spiraling out of control. It's hard to breathe. It's impossible to think. Everything was gone in an instant. Your tears are uncontrollable. Everything you've ever hoped for is incomplete. All that you've believed in and hoped for feels like it's been in vain.

We know the first few days and weeks following your miscarriage or loss are beyond overwhelming. Emotions are hard to predict; feelings are fragile, delicate at best, and the future seems uncertain. The hopes and dreams of expanding your family and all of the joy that comes with it have seemed to vanish. The rug has been pulled out from under you, and you now find yourself navigating through the unknown. We want you to know that you can get there. You can navigate this. You can get to the next day. The next moment. We believe in you.

If this is your first loss, we are here to say there is no right or wrong way to begin the process of picking up the pieces. Instead of telling you what is right or wrong, we'll just tell you that there is a way. A way to survive this. You CAN and WILL move forward. All three of us agree that there are things we probably would've done differently immediately after our loss.

We aren't here to tell you we made all the right decisions. We are here to offer support. We are here to help you gain confidence and assurance that you can get through these first few days and weeks. That all these complex emotions don't have to be debilitating. We are here to offer some tools to help make that process more bearable. As women who have suffered loss, we want to reassure you that you are not alone and that you can do this.

Surviving the right after seems impossible. We know. We thought the same thing. But we are telling you it IS possible. It is survivable. You can do this. You must do it. It is the best gift you can give your child who is no longer on Earth. You can give them a story and carry them in your heart forever. Choose to survive the right after.

Love, Laurel, Kelvi, and Janelle

Surviving Your Relationship with Yourself

I just don't know what this all means. How can I not take responsibility—how can I laugh again or move forward? How can I make it each day when it feels like I shouldn't? I cried out to you. Lord—I've lost my heart. I'm sitting on empty promises. I'm lost and worn out, frustrated, and aching. I want my little guy.

—Janelle's journal entry, week 2

Things I blame myself for: 1. Karaline.

—Kelvi's journal entry, month 8

THE LOSS OF A CHILD is painful. No matter the age, the length of term, or the size of the baby. No matter how many losses you've been through or what stage of pregnancy the loss happens at. Not birthing a child that you were supposed to carry full-term and deliver into the world is a pain like no other.

As the life-providing vessel to your child, your pain and guilt greatly increases your heartache if you blame yourself for the loss. It is hard and maybe even impossible not to blame yourself for some or all of this loss. If I hadn't "worked so much," "lifted all of that," "rested more," "listened to my body and counted the kicks"—these are all quotes from one of us. Words we uttered then and sometimes even now. Words that we know can't change the outcome but have our hearts and our minds wondering, "What if?" Living with yourself daily after your body has failed your child is one of the hardest things to survive.

The accusations you cast upon yourself and the guilt you feel can wreak havoc on your mental well-being. They can make you spiral out of control and into a deep state of depression. The hate you can have for yourself and the immense pain you can feel for taking ownership of this loss is debilitating. But please, don't stay in that place. It is a *part* of the journey, but it is *not* the final destination on your path. It is not a place to stay.

That doesn't mean you can or should try to avoid this part of your journey. Don't shy away from this feeling of guilt and ownership and the work that goes with it. Recognize it for what it is. It's a feeling. It's part of the grief process. It's human nature to blame yourself. In fact, when you have feelings come on you, allow those feelings to come. Let those feelings manifest and be a part of your day. But only let them be a *part* of your day, not *all* of your day. Feelings can be heavy and hard. They can be overwhelming and crushing. But they are also so helpful in the surviving process. Just don't let those feelings become harmful actions. Do not act on those difficult, heavy feelings if those actions will bring you or anyone around you harm. Feelings are just indicators, not dictators. They should not dictate your actions or control what you do; they are valuable insights into the care you need. Feelings are there to bring awareness that your mind and your body are in need of care.

Kelvi remembered feeling embarrassment and shame that her body had let her down. "My body was forced into labor by a placental abruption. I wondered how a healthy woman's body could betray her so badly. I also recall feeling like I had let my husband down by not carrying this baby to full-term."

Laurel went through a lot of self-doubt and kept replaying things she did at work that could have potentially harmed her first pregnancy. Did she expose herself to something at work that would have led to her miscarriage at nine weeks? Did she jeopardize the life of her unborn baby which she should have been protecting with all her might? At the time, they were vaccinating a lot of heifers against brucellosis, which was a zoonotic aborting disease—had she somehow been careless while handling the vaccine? She had also performed a two-hour-long cesarean section and gastropexy on a giant-breed dog with a dystocia—was the anesthesia gas somehow leaking back into the surgery room? There were so many should-haves and could-haves running through her head with no clear answers as to whether they could have caused problems. With all her subsequent pregnancies, Laurel was determined to protect herself at work to keep her baby safe, and she also became a mother hen to her employees who were expecting in the future.

Take the time you need to feel more in rhythm with this new journey.

DURING THIS TIME of surviving yourself, you may begin to feel like you don't want to burden someone else by stepping away from a current role or commitment. From our experiences, if you are feeling this way, we recommend stepping back. Take the time you need to feel more in rhythm with this new journey, the new you that you are becoming. Tell people you need help. Ask them—and *allow* them—to cook dinner for you, clean your house, take the kids to the park. Ask them to pray for you. Communicate the gaps that are occurring in your old self as you embrace your new you. Don't let the feeling of being a burden to others hinder you from asking for more time to heal or taking additional time away from work or commitments.

We understand not wanting to burden others. We were all there at one point or another, but we didn't want to bother anyone. We didn't want to create extra work for anybody else by not going back to work and knowing that our grief and loss and inability to bounce back "quickly" added stress to those around us only made our journeys harder. "I hated not being my old self. I hated not being able to show up at school and just smile and enjoy my students," said Janelle.

We encourage you to take the time you need to heal—and to say aloud that you need that time. Don't be silent about your needs. Share them with your people, share them with yourself. Say what you need and then weigh those needs against your feelings and decide on your next, healthy step to surviving.

Tips for Surviving Yourself

Losing your baby is extremely painful. Losing yourself . . . *that* can be life-altering as well. While there is no one specific combination of tips that will lessen either of these pains, here are suggestions that we found essential in surviving the changes we experienced within ourselves. In an effort to prevent the person you were post-loss from completely disappearing, spend time focusing on one or more of these tips.

Let your feelings come.

Make time for them. Allow your spirit to acknowledge and honor your feelings. Janelle wrote some very emotionally raw words of hurt and anger through the first year of loss. She found this to be key in making it to the next moment and the next day in her journey. On days she tried to avoid or squash her emotions, they'd find a way to flare up with even more intensity.

This is one entry she wrote expressing some of those feelings: "How can we say goodbye before we even said hello? Before we even saw your face, we were planning your headstone. It's not fair. The death of you and the dreams you were to fulfill just rips me apart. How? How does this happen?"

Start a grief journal.

Journaling can be especially helpful if you aren't ready to talk with someone about your emotions or grief. Getting those thoughts and emotions down on paper serves two purposes. First, it allows you to release your emotions externally. This is important because pushing your emotions further and further down only adds fuel to the eventual explosion that is due to erupt at any unexpected moment. Second, you will begin to realize how far you've come and how much growth you've made, both emotionally and spiritually, as you look back over your journal entries.

If you are struggling to begin your journaling, simply start with writing prompts such as:

- Today I feel sad about . . .
- Today I feel happy about . . .
- People I am grateful for today include . . .
- One thing I am proud of accomplishing today was . . .

You can also begin by making a simple list of things that uplift your heart. Try to list three blessings you are grateful for every day. You may write multiple times a day or not journal for days or weeks, but when you do look back, you will realize you were stronger than you thought and made it through some dark times.

Be gentle with yourself.

Don't expect too much of yourself. You're allowed to feel accomplished if all you did for the day was shower. Maybe the next day you'll be able to shower and take out the trash.

Give yourself some grace and allow yourself to slowly engage in the things you want to do. Instead of spending the day focusing on your sense of hurt and loss, allow the Lord to bless you with the grace to believe that what lies ahead will glorify Him and help heal you. And focus on the fact that by releasing your hurt and loss to the Lord, you *did* do something worthwhile for the day.

Take some alone time.

Try going on a long walk, exercising, starting a new hobby, picking up an old one, or even challenging yourself to learn something new. Making time for yourself isn't selfish; it's an important step toward survival. This is a time to spend on yourself. It is a time for you to heal from the inside out.

Exercise sparks endorphins, and endorphins stimulate the brain, so doing something that moves your body or brings a sense of joy is good. Find a short, ten-minute time span and walk your neighborhood. Find a quick exercise link to follow and do it.

While being alone may feel scary, remind yourself that those are just feelings and you need to do things for yourself to find healing. Don't do everything alone, but do find some "you" time.

Breathe.

Take on yoga or meditation. There are wonderful links and internet channels that offer great meditation opportunities. One of the key elements with meditation is to let the meditation help you feel your grief but to not be overwhelmed by it.

If meditation has an uncomfortable component or the practice of yoga doesn't align with your beliefs, find a stretching regimen that suits you. Your body needs to heal from this intense grief, and stretching adds oxygen to your muscles and brain, helping you heal.

Do an activity that draws you close to your baby.

Janelle found herself wanting to draw closer to Eli by doing things from early on in her pregnancy that made her feel connected to him. She would hold his baby blanket. She'd sit outside. She'd visit the cemetery. She'd drink a Coke. All things that made her feel closer to him.

> *"Cradling your little blanket today with such a broken heart was an outward sign of the longing to be holding you. Rocking and cradling the dreams and thoughts of you. Dreams that have disappeared. But in its warmth and softness I find a connection and a bit of comfort. That little blanket held your body for only a moment and today it held my heart and softened this hard day."*

—week 1

I know I need to trust the Lord's timing, but I just feel behind and disappointed.

Throw away your timelines.

Perhaps in your mind, your timeline of having perfectly spaced-out children just got ruined, or perhaps you think you now have to wait for another season to get pregnant because the baby won't be born at just the right time. We understand those pressures. Janelle felt like her and her husband were now "behind" in their family timeline. She wrote, "I hate that I wasted 9½ months. I hate not knowing what went wrong. I hate that there is an empty place in our family line. And that our family isn't whole. I know I need to draw strength in the Lord and trust His timing, but for now I just feel behind and disappointed."

All of that pressure can subside if you work hard to release your expectations and set your carefully laid-out plans aside for the time being. Just be in the here and now, and know that God knows what's best for us in each season.

Set goals for yourself.

When you realize your feelings aren't lessening or going away, set a goal for yourself. If you want a way to handle your feelings differently, you may need to refocus your attempts each day. Start small and build upon that goal. At one time, Janelle tried to start too many goals and activities at once. She wrote, "I've struggled with the balance of letting in the grief and starting new things. I've ignored my grief and thrown myself into activities and it all came crashing down. I know time needs to be given to my grief, but How, When, Where?" Looking back, she realized she didn't set achievable goals. So, set a goal but be realistic about that goal.

It might be that you set a goal to tuck your other children in every night. As the bedtime approaches, set reminders for yourself in your phone that this is something you want to prioritize. You want to work at achieving this goal even while facing the deep pain and grief. So do it. Make every effort to try. If the first night doesn't work, don't dwell on the missed goal. Tell yourself to try again the next night. Even if only part of your goal was met, consider it a victory.

Maybe you want to set a goal to pray more or to read one new book. Then do that. Put a reminder in your phone or on your calendar. Write that goal on your mirror in a dry-erase marker. Leave your Bible out on your counter or nightstand. Be intentional about your goal. Make an effort toward your goal. Be intentional and realistic in your goal.

By finishing a goal or by completing a plan, you are focusing on something other than that deep grief. And when your brain is focused on tasks that aren't as easily consumed by your emotions, a shift starts to happen and natural chemicals are released in your body that aid in your healing journey.

Laurel spent much of her first Christmas season immersed in baking. While it was a mindless task to keep her busy, her kitchen and baking Christmas treats for her neighbors gave her a goal and something to focus on.

You can absolutely make a difference in your grief journey by choosing to focus on goals and outcomes. And when you focus on outcomes and steps forward you can see that good exists, even in your pain. Don't focus on what you wanted to happen; focus on what you can do now. Surviving yourself may just be the biggest battle you fight. It takes time, it takes attention. It takes a willingness to see things from a different point of view. So arm yourself with tools and take every effort to survive yourself.

Janelle wrote, "There have been so few easy days lately. But when they come, those easy days give me some comfort and confidence. It's a chance to look at my precious Eli's pictures and not cry. Or to share those pictures with someone else and not lose complete control. Those easy days almost play an evil trick on me: I feel ready to take another step forward, but then . . . a hard day. A day in which my heart takes over and every moment is excruciatingly painful. Just thinking about my little boy gone ignites a flare in me and sends me into a tailspin of pain. All days are good days from God, but some of those good days are hard. So God, please send me some more easy days."

RECAP

Surviving Your Relationship with Yourself

Surviving yourself may just be the biggest battle you'll fight on this journey. It takes time and attention. It takes a willingness to see things from a different point of view.

Here is a quick recap of tools and thoughts to help you survive yourself.

- Let your feelings come.
- Start a grief journal.
- Be gentle with yourself.
- Don't expect too much of yourself.
- Take some alone time.
- Breathe.
- Do an activity that draws you close to your baby.
- Throw away your timelines.
- Set goals for yourself.

Surviving the Scope of Depression

For the last four days, I will get a glimpse of feeling like my old self. It usually happens in spurts, but then I start to think about the baby and my chest hurts. It is hard to breathe.

—Kelvi's journal entry, April 30, 2019, month 4

NAVIGATING YOUR EMOTIONAL AND MENTAL HEALTH after your loss can be downright exhausting and sometimes disappointing. There are statistics say that up to 20 percent of women experience depression symptoms after miscarriage, and in a majority of those affected, symptoms persist for one to three years, impacting quality of life and subsequent pregnancies.

For the three authors of this book, that statistic is 100 percent.

"About six months after my loss, I recall lying on the floor of my living room on a beautiful summer day. My street was well-known for having dozens of kids running around and parents outside socializing and playing games with some of the kids. I could hear my kids out front playing in the yard, and my husband was also outside enjoying the beautiful weather. But I could not even get myself to move. It was paralyzing. I just lay there and kept blaming myself for my loss. If only my body wouldn't have failed me, or if only I had stopped working and gone on bed rest. I lay there, blaming myself not only for that but for not even being able to go outside and be the mom I'm supposed to be," Kelvi recalled.

In our opinion, the first step to gaining back your mental health is talking about it. You do not have to suffer in silence. Finding another individual you can share your emotions with and getting the right advice can be extremely challenging. Factors such as money, time, and proximity can stop you from finding or seeking out help. Nevertheless, finding the right person is so extremely important. If you have already found a great mental health coach or psychologist, you are ahead of the game. Many women struggle to find the right person, or don't know where to start.

Let's start with psychologists. There are so many to choose from that the process of finding one can be overwhelming. When Kelvi finally admitted to her depression and started looking for a psychologist, she filled out online questionnaires for some offices while searching for the best doctor around. "I was very honest on my questionnaires when shopping for a psychologist," she said. "I was at the point where I knew I needed to do something. I was hesitant to try medication, so I was really looking for someone who could help me navigate my feelings and try to work through my emotions rather than suppress them. The process was life-changing. I met with a psychologist who wanted me to put in the hard work of talking about my emotions, what the outcome of my emotions should look like, and how to get there. It was hard work, but worth it." This is not to say that taking medication is at all bad, but for Kelvi, she wanted to try to navigate the loss without it.

For Janelle, prescription medicine was not part of her immediate healing process. In fact, it was almost one year after losing Eli that she decided to visit her primary care physician. She was still struggling daily to be present and not overcome by uncontrollable emotions. She had a difficult time processing information and completing tasks. And on the advice of her doctor, she began a low dose of antidepressants. She used them to level out the swings of big emotions. To relieve pressure. To make her feel less emotional and less out of control. And it did. She found the right dose of the right medication, and it allowed her to "breathe" a bit more. It allowed her to finish a day without tears and to move forward daily. Medication *can* make a difference, but it was only part of Janelle's toolkit.

Laurel used melatonin and doxylamine to combat severe insomnia as part of her survival journey. She would use these medications to try and help her fall asleep at night, only to wake up going through the whole process of losing Forrest over and over again. Laurel didn't recognize she had depression until much later, when she looked back and noticed she was out of a fog. She just kept thinking, *I'm not happy.* She was a mindless, blank page, just going through the motions every day. After this realization, Laurel started using a HappyLight while she got ready in the morning to help her feel better and improve her depression.

More Practical Ways To Find Help

There are other struggles involved in finding the right mental health coach—so let's talk about money. To be honest, the right mental health counselor or psychologist can be expensive. If paying several hundreds of dollars for a licensed psychologist will put your family in a crunch and add to your guilt, here are some tips for finding help within reasonable means:

Research Catholic Charities USA.

You do not need to be Catholic to receive services from Catholic Charities USA. The Dominican Sisters of Peace is one example of a retreat the organization can connect you with where you can find inner peace, spirituality, and healing. Their services for healing include everything from overnight spirituality retreats to massage therapy to Bible studies and more. Typically, you will be matched one-on-one with a nun who will pray for you and meet with you for individual sessions of therapy and healing.

"Shortly after my loss, a caring woman in our small town gifted me a visit to the Dominican Sisters of Peace in Great Bend," said Kelvi. "At first, I was hesitant to go because the thought of visiting the convent for the day was not really exciting to say the least. Not only that, but as a Lutheran, I was worried about the obvious fact that I didn't fit into the Catholic traditions and religion. However, shortly after I arrived, I felt an immense sense of peace and healing. I met and prayed one-on-one with my counselor, ate lunch with the nuns, had a massage, and spent time alone in the library for journaling and reflection. I left the convent feeling the most at peace that I had felt since my loss. The Sister I was matched with is still a great friend and periodically checks in with me to see how I am doing. The experience was so impactful that I later passed along this sweet gift to another individual who was going through a hard time."

Reach out to your church pastor.

Perhaps you don't feel comfortable doing this or don't currently attend a church. That is okay. Many areas have a ministerial alliance in which area churches will work together to find assistance for you. If you are a member of a hometown church, your pastor may have resources available to you. Those resources may be either online or in print.

If visiting with a pastor or getting those materials is too uncomfortable in a face-to-face setting, then send an email to a local church asking for online correspondence. Someone at the church may also be able to connect you to a community or outreach organization that can help.

Reach out to another mother who's suffered a loss similar to yours.

What a beautiful gift you can be to someone encountering a loss such as yours. Those relationships can help you both. Offer to take her to coffee or have her over for a visit. No one is more capable of being a listening ear and offering guidance than someone else who has walked in their shoes. Beautiful friendships and relationships can be built out of loss. Healing can happen for both parties. It can be therapeutic. In fact, the three of us were brought together because we reached out to one another after our losses.

Janelle's husband, Kirk, carves beautiful "Joy" rocks out of limestone. They give these rocks as gifts to mothers after they hear of their miscarriage or infant loss. It is a simple way to let others know that they are not alone.

The "Joy" rock that Kirk and Janelle gift to other moms of loss

Tips for Surviving Depression

Although meeting with your mental health counselor or friend can be extremely helpful, it is not always easy to find the time. Or even worse yet, you may be unable to meet with your counselor when you are having a bad day or in a low. We each experienced that in some way or another. Finding time to get support or check in with a health care specialist or a friend was difficult.

Here are some helpful tips to get through the bad days when you just can't seem to get out of bed or shake those bitter emotions:

Don't be idle.

Seems easy, right? Not so much when you are overcome with emotion. But very simply put, you need to get active. Get yourself out of bed. Take a shower, go for a walk, go out into your yard and do some yard work—whatever it takes, but don't be idle.

If you live in a friendly climate, plant a garden or try to conquer a local hiking trail. If the thought of physical activity now makes you cringe, start easier.

Go to your local library and scan the book sections. Find yourself a book or two. What we found as mothers of loss is that resources and materials for those struggling with miscarriages, stillbirth, and infant loss aren't always readily available. Books on this topic were limited or nonexistent. So if you can't find something that speaks to your emotional needs, ask your librarian for a recommendation. You may not be ready to read specifically about infant loss just yet, so ask them to direct you toward something marketed as "light and easy" or "uplifting." When you are struggling through overwhelming emotions, you can get pulled into that "you are what you think" mentality, so a lighthearted book may help you start to think about yourself differently. Janelle picked up an emotionally beautiful book by Kris Power titled *Battle Cry: Hope and Healing in the Battles of Life*. While reading Kris's story broke her heart, Janelle found herself connecting to the roller coaster of emotions and the depth of emotions Kris poured into her story. Some of those words and phrases became mantras for Janelle, and she credits some of her healing to reading and hearing others' stories. Find books that lift you up.

Volunteer for a day with a local charity.

There are many organizations that can use an extra hand. Call your local chamber of commerce and ask what groups may need assistance for an hour or two. If that sounds like too much, see if they could use any help with distributing flyers or a small local project. Not only will these activities help you stop constantly thinking about your loss, but you will also feel better for contributing to your community. You'll be reaping the rewards of your new garden, the physical activity, or the gratitude from others you helped.

In the first year after her loss, Janelle organized and led a small candlelight vigil on October 15, Pregnancy and Infant Loss Remembrance Day. She posted on a social media site that a gathering was going to happen in the local park—a gathering to remember children gone too soon. She invited anyone who wanted to come and remember families who had suffered loss. It was an opportunity to offer support and to bring awareness to the statistic that each year, more than 26,000 babies in the United States are born still and over one million pregnancies end in miscarriage. Candles were lit. A prayer was read. Music was played. Silence was had. Intentional silence. And for those brief 15 minutes, Janelle brought awareness to the community and a time for comfort to families and friends grieving.

Challenge yourself.

Start easy, but try learning something new. Whether that is speaking a new language, playing the piano, or making your own sourdough bread, challenge yourself.

Remember, you don't have to master everything at once. If you want to learn to play the piano, sit down and try to play a simple song to start. If you are ready for more, check out some online piano tutorial sites and enroll in some lessons. If you want in-person interactive time, schedule lessons with a piano instructor.

You might challenge yourself to read a chapter of the Bible every week, then research the historical context that shaped that chapter. If you do not already have a study Bible, now is a great time to get one. So much can be gained by reading the context behind different chapters.

Another example could be learning a new language. Download Rosetta Stone or Duolingo or listen to podcasts. Better yet, include your family or spouse in your learning journey, and pretty soon you might be conversing over dinner in a new language.

By challenging yourself, you put purpose back into your days and allow yourself to start feeling confident in your accomplishments. While some of these challenges may seem counterproductive or meaningless, they actually provide opportunities for your brain to veer away from emotional thinking and focus on logical, methodical learning.

If challenging yourself with something new is too overwhelming, at least make an effort to return to something you've done before. For Janelle, that was writing and directing the annual children's Christmas pageant at her church. That's an activity she's done in the past, so focusing on that familiar event in the years after losing Eli helped her heal.

Find a positive outlet.

Laurel kept herself busy in an attempt to not think about her loss. She baked and baked. She organized photo albums. She immersed herself in purchasing a business partnership and was on call every other night and every other weekend.

"Find a good outlet and focus on it if you need to," Laurel said. "Find something that helps you express your hurt, your love, your grief. I normally love singing, but I couldn't get myself to sing anything for over a year after losing Forrest. I just listened to a Volbeat song on repeat while driving around. I blasted that song on my really bad days. I also kept Christmas music playing for as long as I could because that's what was on the radio when we lost Forrest. I was holding on to memories and not wanting to forget."

Outlets can be any of those things we mentioned with challenging yourself. But they can also be sewing, photography, or even painting. Use your creative brain and produce something positive. Manifest something positive.

Stop overuse of alcohol and/or drugs.

It is easy to numb feelings with alcohol or drugs. A glass of wine postpartum can lead to two, then three, and pretty soon, the whole bottle. Alcohol is a natural depressant. Not only will you wake up feeling your depression at a deeper level, but you will add the physical side effects of alcohol. The same can be said about many drugs. We are not saying you cannot drink alcohol or use prescription drugs appropriately. But the key is knowing your limit and sticking to it.

Perhaps a drink or two at night does not affect your mood. Perhaps you use that time to connect with your husband or simply relax after a long day. We are not here to tell you that is not okay. But be wise and intentional in your use of alcohol while healing from loss. We do encourage you to give up drugs and alcohol first in an effort to "grow" through the emotions rather than suppress them for another day.

Sometimes, your body becomes used to a certain routine or habit. Perhaps your body is used to a glass of wine or a beer in the evening. Your brain may be programmed to say, "Okay, it's 7 p.m.—time for that drink." Or your mind says, "It's time to take that pill." Breaking that habit first is the key to stopping overuse of drugs or alcohol. It seems silly, but our bodies even get accustomed to actual physical habits at certain times of the day. Your body may think it's time for the physical activity of lifting the glass to your mouth.

If you are struggling to break a habit of drinking, start by replacing the drink with a nonalcoholic drink so that the physical motion of bringing a glass to your mouth doesn't also have to be replaced. Now, to be clear, replacing one bad habit with another bad habit is only a temporary solution. Replacing your drink with a soda or ice cream shake isn't ideal, but it might be a good starting point. A healthier approach could be finding a substitute that you can start with or work toward, such as sparkling cider, and go from there.

Drugs can have similar effects as alcohol. They reprogram your brain to need or depend on a substance. Whether that is abusing prescription medications or overusing marijuana, misuse of drugs can derail your healing. Avoidance of your pain is not found in any sort of drug, legal or illegal.

Make a checklist of tasks to accomplish in one day.

Making a checklist may seem silly and easy, but focusing on a checklist and not solely on your feelings can allow your brain the space to do some healing. Following your checklist allows you to shift your attention to the next task, and then the next, rather than allowing yourself to wallow in despair and grief. Your brain may not be able to focus on what to do next in a systematic approach without a list like this.

For Janelle, her trauma brain left her with gaps of unremembered moments. "Sometimes I'd go through a day or a conversation and would walk away not remembering what was said, or I'd have said things all wrong. I was almost in a fog." Following a checklist may help you focus on your daily needs as well as help you clear the fog. But again, start simple and build on it.

For example, day one may just look like this:

- Shower
- Get dressed
- Read the Bible
- Put away dishes
- Cook dinner

By the end of the week or month, hopefully you've accomplished those items and possibly added some enrichment activities: volunteer to walk dogs at the shelter, start a new Bible study, offer to read to kids at a daycare center, or join a church group.

Take proper care of your body's physical needs.

This is the same advice you read everywhere, right? Well, that's because it is a key piece of your survival journey, to getting your mental health back on track.

We've found that at a time like this, your body needs to move—so move! Take a walk, dance to a special song, jog. It wasn't until after the first year of her loss that Janelle started to move. It took her time to get to that place. But starting in August of 2015, she challenged herself to walk to the cemetery every day. No matter the time of day. No matter the weather. Despite her schedule of activities, she'd walk the mile to the cemetery and turn right back around and walk home. For five months, this was her way of keeping Eli in her mind and giving her body purpose. Keep moving your body.

Whatever we put into our bodies is what we get out of our bodies. Just like a broken arm needs a cast, you also need aides to help yourself heal. Both your body and mind need to heal, and that may take exercise, sunshine, and/or supplements. For example, keep a close eye on your iron levels. If lethargy is taking over, it's a good idea to call your OB-GYN's office and ask for a multivitamin that includes iron.

Adding a vitamin D supplement may be an option if getting outside in the sunlight is challenging for you. The average person is low on vitamin D even when getting adequate sunlight exposure, so it may be a great idea to add this to your daily supplements year-round. A blood test at your doctor's office can evaluate your vitamin D levels and tell you exactly what your body needs. What we know is your body and mind need to heal and that may take exercise, sunshine, and/or supplements.

Buy a light therapy lamp.

This light helps to boost mood, increase energy, encourage healthier sleep, and improve focus. Laurel's sister used one to combat the winter blues, and she suggested Laurel buy a HappyLight when she was in the darkest days of her depression. Laurel started by turning on the light in the morning while she was getting ready for work, but she has also used it while stretching in the morning, breastfeeding a baby, or working on paperwork. She continues to use her light therapy lamp during the winter and spring months when her body and mind start to feel sluggish from decreased light exposure.

Get enough proper sleep. Set some limits for your screen time. Turn off the devices for a night and pick up one of the books you grabbed from the library. In an effort to stay in the faith or to begin your faith walk, try reading some Scripture before you fall asleep.

Set boundaries.

It is hard to start feeling better when something or someone is feeding negativity into your life. Social media is usually the first place to start setting boundaries. If you aren't ready to delete your favorite social media site, set some parameters for what you see and read.

Whatever you need to do to set boundaries
for yourself, do it.

For example, if you have a friend who does nothing but complain on Facebook, start by clicking those three little dots in the corner of their page and scroll down to where it says "Snooze for 30 Days." Maybe it's just too overwhelming to see others posting about fun and plans. That's okay. Tap that Unfollow or Snooze button and let your feed be a place of peace instead of frustration. Rebuild your social circle. After the 30-day snooze, the site will give you the option to renew their snooze time or let that person back on your feed. Whatever you need to do to set boundaries for yourself, do it!

We talk more about this in the Relationships section, but for the purpose of feeling better on an off day, remember to turn the phone off and pick up something that brings enrichment. Other boundaries to consider setting are:

- The music you listen to
- What you read
- The friends you choose to spend time with
- Extracurricular groups you volunteer for that take advantage of your time

Remember that what you open the door to, you will receive—both the good and the bad. Be careful of what you are seeking and what you allow yourself to be exposed to.

Go to church.

After our losses, all three of us struggled to get back to our "normal" spirituality. We expand more on this in the section Surviving the Faith, but finding immediate relief does not happen by staying in bed on Sunday morning. Making yourself do hard things enables God's Spirit to live through you and allows the story God is writing about your life to be shown to the world. So get up and go!

Journal.

Writing your feelings down doesn't just allow you to get your emotions out in a safe way; it also allows you to see your growth and progress through this journey. Maybe you are having a hard day or week and you feel like you could explode emotionally. Get out a notebook and start writing all of it down. Don't worry about sequence or structure or anyone else reading it, just start writing. Write about your day or what is currently upsetting you. Write about a relationship that is weighing you down and why. Write it down.

Janelle shares, "Going back through my journals, I can see the difference even in the handwriting between easy days and hard days. On hard days, the strokes are quick and messy. On easy days, there is spacing and less mess. Both types of entries are expressions of love. Even on days when all I could do was draw Eli's name or rewrite a Scripture, writing in my journal helped me heal."

Expressing pain through written words was a saving grace for Janelle. We share some of our journal entries throughout this book so that you can witness the highs and lows in our personal struggles with grief. More importantly, we hope these journal entries will resonate with you or help you understand that you are not alone in feeling the way you do.

At the end of your journal entries, make a list of things you are grateful for today or simply write the names of the people you love. For example: "Today I was grateful for: my friend _____, good weather, and my home."

If you find it a struggle to write and keep a journal, that's okay too! Laurel did not journal during her journey of loss. Writing doesn't come naturally to her, and it didn't offer her comfort. You may find yourself there. Again, whatever strategy you choose to adopt along your grief journey, make it a positive outlet that works for you.

THE TRUTH OF IT IS that processing your emotions and getting the right mental help is hard. It's a hard truth, and acting on that truth can be harder. It takes a lot of work. In reality, at times, it can look like taking one step forward and five steps backward. The important thing is that you continue to take the step forward.

Our society does a great job of talking *around* mental health and framing it more as self-care than self-help. There is a big difference. Sure, a spa day and a pedicure can temporarily make you feel better, but getting to a strong mental state takes time and a lot of work. Don't let the silence win. Take the first step and start talking about how you are feeling.

RECAP

Surviving the Scope of Depression

The truth of it is that processing your emotions and getting the right mental help is hard. It's a hard truth, and doing it can be harder. It takes a lot of work.

- Don't be idle.
- Volunteer for a day with a local charity.
- Challenge yourself.
- Find a positive outlet.
- Stop overuse of alcohol and/or drugs.
- Make a checklist of tasks to accomplish in one day.

- Take proper care of your body's physical needs.
- Buy a light therapy lamp.
- Set boundaries.
- Go to church.
- Journal.

Surviving Guilt and Shame

But the more days that pass, the deeper I hurt, the more I sleep, and the more I withdraw. Help me! Ease my pain, help me find JOY in this.

—Janelle's journal entry, week 1

I not only lost my son this past month but I lost my ability to function appropriately. I lost who I need to be for my family. I panic. I have anxiety attacks at the simplest tasks. I've left my husband to take care of the girls—how unfair. He's forced to carry the load. Because I can't. I just can't. I panic. Things I could do without thinking about them crush me now. They hold me captive. How am I supposed to survive this?

—Janelle's journal entry, day 2

I feel like I failed Karaline.

I am so sad that Kacy won't be a big sister. It would be so fun to see her in that role. Kacy asked me, "Why did our baby have to die?" That bothered me all night.

—Kelvi's journal entries, month 4

TWO OF THE BIGGEST EMOTIONS that drive depression are guilt and shame. Perhaps you feel one of them, or perhaps it's both. Both of these complex feelings need to be addressed.

So let's start with the ugly emotion of guilt in relation to miscarriage or pregnancy loss. If you carry guilt from your loss, we would like to speak these words to you:

---

*There is nothing you could have done differently
to change the outcome of losing your baby.*

For several months and even up until a few years after miscarriage, all three of us continually asked ourselves what we could've done differently to prevent the outcomes we had to face. Feeling like you should've been on bed rest or taken it easier at work is not a place to stay. You can acknowledge those feelings for what they are: untruths.

If you can't let go of the guilt yet, at least let someone else hold that emotion for you. Give that feeling to one of those people who you can consider a burden bearer. Burden bearers are the genuine, honest, soul-lifting people who can listen to your heart and take you at your worst and not pass judgment. They accept your hurt and willingly walk your journey of grief with you. Some burden bearers are friends you've had forever, and some may be people you've just met. Whoever they are, they are fully trustworthy people who allow you to be completely vulnerable.

Janelle was blessed in her journey by several burden bearers, but by far, her colleague and friend-in-faith, Mary Anne, was the person who took her hurt and validated it the most. She spoke Eli's name often and was intentional about checking in on Janelle. For her, Mary Anne was a burden bearer who could take on the weight of Janelle's grief and offer unconditional support. She not only held Janelle's grief in her heart, but she never passed judgment. She was and still is invaluable to Janelle's journey. People like Mary Anne can play key role in your survival. The support from a burden bearer who can take your feelings and the weight of your grief in their hearts for a short time is so impactful in helping you deal with grief. Search for such a person. And as they hold your guilt, you can begin to deal with the second ugly emotion: shame.

Shame can look like many things. Maybe you are shameful for how you feel right now. Please know you should never feel shame for having emotions. Emotions signal that you need to address something in your life. All feelings are valid, so don't feel ashamed for having feelings. Every one of us can and will experience grief differently.

Maybe, however, you are feeling shameful for how you acted after your loss. "Yelling at my mom to get out of my house just weeks after losing Eli was a low point," remembered Janelle. "It was a point at which my feelings were bigger than what I or anyone else could understand. It was a point at which people who didn't understand the pain and heartbreak I was going through didn't know what to do. And when all of those things collided, I found myself in a single moment of frustration, anger, and embarrassment that I am not proud of now." Shame can make you feel like you are not worthy of love, not worthy of relationships. Shame can make you feel deep embarrassment of yourself and how others might see you. "After suffering our second loss through miscarriage, I felt shameful that my body failed me again. I didn't like myself. I felt broken and unworthy. It was hard to even speak about this loss due to the overwhelming feelings of guilt and shame," recalled Janelle.

Kelvi adds that she, too, felt enormous amounts of guilt and shame. "I felt guilty for letting my family down. I felt shame that my body failed to carry this pregnancy. The same day that we lost Karaline, we sat all three of our children down together to tell them what had happened. My children were 9, 7, and 4. I recall my oldest immediately crying. I felt such intense amounts of shame that I let them down and that my failure to carry this pregnancy led to their sadness."

We urge you to remember at the end of the day, you are human. We are humans. We cannot act perfectly, especially when it comes to processing those complex, tough emotions. Complex emotions are hard to handle at any age. What we can do is learn from those feelings and experiences and work at trying to do better.

If you are experiencing shame because you feel as if your emotions shouldn't matter or shouldn't be real, we understand. We want you to hear this from us: your feelings *do* matter. It is so hard when those around you don't recognize your feelings, and it is extremely hard to feel shame about your feelings or how long you've had them. However, one thing we can all three share is this: There is strength in vulnerability. It takes courage to be vulnerable and share that you are feeling deep emotions like grief and shame. As uncomfortable as it is in the short term to express these deep emotions, you will find strengthened relationships with others and personal emotional growth in the long run.

Tips for Surviving Guilt and Shame

When it comes to complex feelings, there is no timeline for grief. It's important to have a few survival tips you can rely on at any stage of your journey. Whether that is the swing of extreme guilt or the embarrassment over your body failing its mom-job, tools to help you manage those complex feelings are essential. This list of suggestions focuses on you surviving the complexity of guilt and shame. All three of us have experienced a level of guilt and shame and believe these suggestions helped us in one way or another.

Acknowledge your feelings and let them get recognition.

Making your feelings known, especially at such a vulnerable time, can be difficult. But even if it is difficult, you need to speak your feelings. The right time and tone for sharing your feelings are essential to being heard and acknowledged, so keep those two things in mind as you seek validation and assert your feelings. And remember, being vulnerable is brave! Being vulnerable with your feelings will ultimately lead to freedom.

Try to speak your peace and deliver your message, but be prepared that some people will not be receptive. Delivering your feelings to a person who is unreceptive will not to be successful. If you find yourself sharing your feelings and being disrespected or disregarded, then be wise and recognize there needs to be a boundary in place with that person.

Your feelings are valid. But not everyone will validate those feelings or validate you. In fact, you may not even know what you are feeling let alone be able to speak those feelings out loud. If you find yourself unable to identify what you need or what you want to say, we understand. Ten years later, Janelle can now recognize that she may not have even been able to express what she needed back then. It's taken her that long to reach point where she can identify what she needs and give those feelings a voice. So while we encourage you to speak out, we also understand that you may not be able to do that. Be patient with yourself if you can't find your voice.

Seek help.

We cannot state this enough: Your mental well-being is not only important to you, but it's important to those around you. Perhaps you have already been blessed with other children who need a mother who is present, or perhaps your spouse is struggling to help you overcome your loss and feels like they need their partner back. It may not seem like it early on, but eventually, with help, you will start to get parts of your "old" self back, and hours will string into days and perhaps even weeks at a time where you can function like you did before.

And don't be afraid to test-drive psychologists or counselors. If you don't feel comfortable talking with someone or you don't feel like it is a good match, you have permission to try out different providers without feeling guilty about it. It may take some time to find the right fit for you and your needs, but once you do, you will know it.

Apologize and forgive.

If you are carrying added guilt or shame for how you treated someone after your loss, give yourself some grace, and then reach out to them and offer an apology. It doesn't need to be long or lengthy, overthought or extravagant; just simply tell that person, "Hey, I am sorry for the things I said while I was grieving my miscarriage," or "You are important to me, and I am sorry if I hurt your feelings over the last few months."

To fight the battle and win takes strength. To live while dying takes more than just understanding. It takes patience and tons of grace.

Then, accept God's forgiveness and offer yourself some grace. None of this is easy and none of it is the same for everyone, but taking the steps to heal yourself and your relationships is something to be proud of. Give yourself the grace you deserve.

Janelle wrote, "So how can one find peace if there's a constant war raging in myself? Deceit, turmoil, angst, worry . . . yet there is love, joy, and grace. All at the same time. To find peace with all of that in your head and heart is enough of a challenge, let alone the daily challenges. To fight the battle and win takes strength. To live while dying takes more than just understanding. It takes patience and tons of grace."

Know your triggers.

Shame can catch you off guard. It can happen when one of your kids asks about their sibling in Heaven or the first time you hold a newborn after your loss. Or perhaps it is having to tell your spouse about yet another negative pregnancy test after you've been trying for so long. Different things will trigger your emotional pain, but we encourage you to face your triggers head-on. Over time, if you continue to meet these situations with the mindset that you can overcome them, each occurrence will become easier to conquer. Communicate with those around you when you feel these emotions start to come on. Stand up for yourself and your feelings using gentle statements with those who may be triggering them. Try to stay calm and help others understand your pain, and that you are trying to get through it. Those who love you will embrace your bravery and help you work through the tough times with more patience and understanding.

Let go of any anger attached to the loss.

It's understandable that you may feel angry after your loss. So many things didn't turn out the way you had hoped. Placing blame on doctors, your work, or worse yet, yourself, can all intensify your anger. But being angry does not change the outcome of losing your baby. It does, however, slow down the healing process or even block the healing process altogether. Allow yourself to feel the emotion of anger, but do not stay in it, and do not act on it. We encourage you to find a healthy way to release anger by acknowledging it, speaking it, and seeking help if you can't get rid of it on your own.

Kelvi added, "For months, I was angry with God that He even had me get pregnant in the first place. I would ask, 'If you knew how this would end, why would you even allow me to carry this baby? Why not save me the despair?'" We aren't promised that life will be easy. What we are promised is that God will never leave us while we go through tough times. And we believe that truth for ourselves and for you.

Find comfort in Scripture.

For all three of us, our comfort and truth lies in what God reminds us in His word. The Bible tells us that "in his hand is the life of every living thing and the breath of all mankind" (Job 12:10). God created your baby for a reason. God also decided when to call that sweet baby to his or her heavenly home. In Psalm 139:16, we hear, "Your eyes saw my unformed substance; in your book were written every one of them, the days that were formed for me, when as yet there was none of them." It was decided when that baby was conceived how many days he or she would live, whether in the womb or not. It is time to let go of the "shoulda, coulda, woulda" mantras, no matter how hard that is. And it is hard to get past the guilt. But it is important to understand that for everything, there is a season.

RECAP

Surviving Guilt and Shame

It takes courage to be vulnerable and share that you are feeling such deep emotions like grief and shame. As uncomfortable as it is in the short term to express these deep emotions, you will find strengthened relationships with others, and personal growth emotionally in the long run, if you can be honest about your feelings.

- Acknowledge your feelings and let them get recognition.

- Seek help.

- Apologize and forgive.

- Know your triggers.

- Let go of any anger attached to the loss.

- Find comfort in Scripture.

Surviving When Your Faith
Seems to Be Failing

Don't let me forget, Lord, let me hold tight to the promises and hold on to the memories. Let me not forget the love and compassion of others. Let me feel with my heart all the glories around me. May I remember how to comfort others in the same way in which you are comforting me.

—2 Corinthians 13–4

Let me remember wholly my little guy and let me use it as a ministry to others.

—Janelle's journal entry, week 1

What am I now . . . not a widow, not an orphan . . . just a momma without her child. But I also know . . . that I am a child of God. That I am a loved sister, an honored teacher, mother, and friend. So my heart is still rejoicing in all of that—but I still ache. I still sit wondering what I am now. Help me rest and not feel like I need to know what is next and to be okay with not having a plan.

—Janelle's journal entry, week 2

I feel like Satan has his claws in me and is trying to tear me down.

—Kelvi's journal entry, month 8

ONE TOOL we encourage you to have or possibly just rekindle in the first days after your loss is FAITH! Faith, as a tool, is immeasurable in your survival. Simply put, faith is the biggest comfort you can have when nothing else in the world can truly ease the pain of such a loss.

As Christians, we three authors encourage you to believe in Jesus Christ. We are praying for you to come to know Him and follow Him and have Him be the foundation on which you live daily. We want nothing more for you than to know the comfort God can give you through belief in Him, albeit sometimes in the smallest of amounts during your loss. We share our faith journeys through our Christian convictions. At the end of this section, you'll find tools for your faith journey, as well as Scripture verses that offer quick reassurances of hope in Jesus Christ.

Whether you are new to faith, your belief in God is wavering, or you've never met the Lord in your heart, it's okay. It's not too late to make faith a key element to your survival. Simply put, faith is just a strongly held belief—a belief in something or someone greater than our here and now. It is a confidence that surpasses human understanding of pain and pleasure, success and failure. It is a trust, a conviction; it's an ever-present nugget we can cling to, lean on, surround ourselves with, and even come back to if we've lost our way. Faith is essential to surviving your loss.

All three of us found our spiritual lives altered and changed during our survival-of-loss journey. There were times we faced the inability to pray. Times we couldn't even say what was on our hearts because our hearts couldn't feel anything except immense sadness. There were times when overwhelming emptiness made it difficult to sit in the pew at church. There were weeks on end when we found ourselves skipping services or being absent-minded about worship. Those days were just too hard.

Recognizing the likelihood that your spiritual life will change will help you become more in touch with your faith. Spending time reading Scripture or talking to an elder, a minister, or your priest keeps you connected to your core—the core that establishes your life choices and spiritual decisions. It keeps you connected to your chosen faith. Find a devotional that speaks life into you and into your daily walk. If you can't find a prayer or utter a praise to God, then just speak what's on your heart as if you are talking aloud to yourself. Let it go into the space around you. Let it be said, all of it: the good, the easy, the hard, the confusion, the hate. Say it all. Even if it doesn't feel like a prayer, talk out loud to God. Share your raw emotions and face the change that comes on the new path of faith in loss.

Don't expect yourself to get to and understand this new space overnight. It takes time. Don't put pressure on yourself that you should be "better" by now, or that you should be exactly the way you were before—nothing is the same, and you need time. Just as where you were with your spirituality before your loss didn't evolve overnight, this part of your "new you" won't develop overnight either.

Grace is a powerful thing to give yourself. Give yourself grace. Give yourself time for prayer. Time for healthy words that breathe life into the dark hole you now have in your heart. Grace and prayer and hope. And, of course, a good friend or two.

Kelvi recalled, "Before my miscarriage, I considered my faith to be both active and strong. I rarely missed a Sunday church service, I attended Bible studies and adult Sunday School on a weekly basis, and my prayer life was very active. In fact, most mornings after my family left the home, you'd find me on my hands and knees praying over them and giving thanks to God for His many blessings. In the evenings, we prayed together as a family of five, and after our group prayer, I would pray alone in my bed before I fell asleep.

"But immediately after my miscarriage, that faith and my prayer life fell silent. 'Why would a God so good cause something so bad to happen to one of his children? Why would He take Karaline from me? Why would He have me get pregnant if He knew how this would turn out?' These questions were on repeat, and I began to wonder if the same God I'd trusted my whole life had turned His back on me. Days began to pass without me praying, and that soon turned into weeks.

"I recall many mornings yearning to have my old prayer life back and trying to pray, but the words were completely gone. I would go through the motions of getting down on my hands and knees in my bedroom only to just be sitting there in total silence. Not only were the words not there, but more concernedly, my heart wasn't either. My complete confidence and trust in Jesus was hanging on by a thread."

Laurel most definitely used to be a God-fearing woman. After losing Forrest, though, she simply lost faith. She couldn't find the words to pray, reference God, or participate in church; she was so disturbed about her faith just seeming to disappear overnight. Had it not been for her husband, Bryce, carrying her through all those Sunday mornings, she may not have found herself back in church. She felt like a blank page. For her, losing Forrest was a "freak accident," so she wasn't mad at God; she wasn't mad at anyone. She was just empty. She took steps to try to feel her faith again and to keep believing. She visited with her priest to see when she would return to "normal," and while he directed her toward some books to read about grief, he also didn't know when her faith would return. He just knew it would take work and time. Slowly, day by day, Laurel's faith has been getting stronger, and working on her faith is something she is still doing to this day.

Janelle shared that her prayer life after her loss was deepened. She cried out to God in the easy and hard times. She would rewrite Scripture and jot down prayers and praises. She sought after God's answers and His peace. She prayed for comfort. She prayed for calm and understanding. Janelle wrote prayers of anger and sadness. She turned to her faith for strength.

"My faith life and prayer life weren't unwavering, though they were. I internally fought the battle between reaching out to God and wanting to be distant from Him. I wrote prayers and petitions to Christ for mercy and encouragement. I prayed for Him to be present because He felt distant. I wavered on the line of wanting to know God and His plan and wanting to turn my back and walk away. The one thing that remained constant in all of my journaling was that even when I was struggling with faith and fears, I did continue to seek Him. Seeking Him for understanding, healing, help, seeking to know Him deeper, all while pleading with Him to take the pain, might not make any sense, but it sure was the raw truth of what I was needing."

As Christians, we are not excluded from the disappointments and experiences that can test one's faith. However, God always gives us a lifeline to grab on to.

As Christians, we are not excluded from the disappointments and experiences that can test one's faith. Never in the Bible does God promise our earthly lives will be free from heartache or despair. However, what God does always offer us is the way out. He gives us a lifeline to grab on to. A lifeline who was human Himself and suffered immense despair on a cross: Jesus Christ. Jesus may be carrying you along or offering you His helping hand out of the deep, dark depth of depression, despair, heartache, and temptation. And not only that; He has promised to never leave our side while we are there.

The Gospel can be summed up in four words: *God gives, we receive.* If you are struggling to find your way out of grief, depression, or sadness, all you have to do is open your heart to Him. Grab on to the lifeline that God gives us through His son, Jesus. You can do this by receiving Him through His Word. Start by opening up your Bible. If you were like Laurel and were so grief-stricken you couldn't bring yourself to read, then return to your church family to just sit and listen to the Word of the Lord spoken to you. Within the fellowship of believers, you can find love, unity, loyalty, and strength in numbers. If you do not have a church family, ask God to open a door for you to find one.

Janelle chose to journal, seek spiritual companions, find solitude, visit with her pastor, and turn her grief into purpose. Laurel prayed a lot of rosaries to fill her blank mind; she prayed them while driving, working, cooking supper, and cleaning the house. She heavily relied on the *Mary, Undoer of Knots* novena to help her get through the grief and said many prayers in her *Mother Love* prayer book for Christian mothers.

"As for me and my faith journey, it took a few years to uproot that seed of doubt and resentment from my heart," said Kelvi. "But what got me there was returning to church on Sunday mornings, reading my Bible, and challenging myself by reading Christian-based books and listening to podcasts that preached salvation through Jesus. I grew *in* my faith and not away from it."

Being a God-fearing woman doesn't mean you don't doubt. It doesn't mean your faith walk is unaffected by circumstance. Being a God-fearing woman actually allows you the grace to fall apart and know that God still holds you in His palms. He will never not love you. He will never leave you—even when you are absent from church, your pew, or your normal daily prayer life.

Tips for Surviving When Your Faith Is Wavering

When it feels like the foundation of your belief that keeps you hopeful in desperate times is gone, you are going to have to fight for it. You have to put in work to survive this.

Find a spiritual companion.

Surround yourself with Christians. Do not feel guilty for calling on each other when you are feeling down or alone. Brothers and sisters in Christ are called to pray for one another and bind up one another's wounds.

After Janelle's loss, a women's group from another local church called her and asked if they could stop by and visit her. Janelle shared, "Their group brought over toiletries and coloring books for my girls. They sat in my living room one evening and offered to pray for me. They prayed for Eli. They prayed for comfort and strength and peace. They listened to Eli's delivery story. They cried while I cried. They were silent when I was silent. They listened. That small group of women planted themselves in my journey that night and have forever been imprinted in my heart because of that. What they did helped me." Being with other Christians is a beautiful gift you can give yourself on this journey.

If Christianity is foreign to you, find your "faith group of people," the ones who lift you up to the greater you. The people who both challenge you and speak words of life into you. Find those brave, bold friends who build you up and help you survive.

The three of us would not be true to our calling as Christians if we didn't tell you the absolute truth: Jesus Christ is the Way, the Truth, and the Life. And through Him, you will be saved. So if you are not a Christian, we pray for you to find God, not only to walk with you in that journey but to carry you now and into the weeks and months and years to come. Jesus is the ultimate Christian companion.

Gravitate toward burden bearers.

We previously mentioned burden bearers. They are the soul-supporting people who can take your pain and fear, your doubts and hurt, all your feelings, and hold them for you for a while. They are the people you pour your soul out to, and they don't judge you or gossip about you. They just take your burdens and keep them for you for a time. They are willing to pray for you and for your burdens. They are trustworthy and understanding people who are helping you through your loss. Burden bearers can be your pastor or priest, or they can be elders or deacons in your church. They can be Sunday school teachers, youth leaders, or interim pastors. Or they can be a family member, lifelong friend, or perhaps even a new friend who, over time, you realize you can trust to hold your feelings and encourage you to keep stepping forward in your path to healing.

Make time for prayer.

Be intentional about praying. Pray as often as you can; start with simple words of thankfulness after a good part of your day and expand upon that.

If you can't find the words, state a generic prayer, or just utter words that are in your heart. But don't stop talking to God.

Pray the Book of Psalms in the Bible. It may be difficult to express your emotions to God. The Book of Psalms allows us to join with God in joy, hope, sorrow, and fear. It lets us take His words and speak them back to Him in order to soften our hearts and reconnect with Him when we can't find the words. If you need help getting started, there are several free, downloadable guides online, or you can simply start with Psalm 1 and read five Psalms a day for 30 days.

Pick up or start a spiritual discipline.

Meditation, hospitality, solitude, and journaling are all good spiritual practices. If you are uncertain what each one means, take time to research them. Find out what each entails and how they help your spiritual growth. Pick a discipline to try. Then talk to your spiritual companion and help them to hold you accountable in that discipline. This is another opportunity to redirect your brain from emotional thinking to practical application.

If you attend church regularly, do not stop.

As easy as it may be to skip your weekly worship service, it's a win for Satan if you stop going. Continuing to go to church may be hard at first, especially if you felt like Laurel—empty and blank—or Janelle—crushed and downhearted—or Kelvi, whose convictions were in question. Eventually, that pain will ease, and getting back into your weekly routine will become natural.

Janelle's pastor was not only a Christian companion; she would do check-ins with her if Janelle had missed a weekly service. At one point, Janelle recalled her pastor showing up on her porch and saying she hadn't seen Janelle in church for three weeks. She told Janelle that she was missed at worship. Her pastor was an integral part of her healing. We truly believe that even if you feel disassociated in your weekly worship, God is still planting seeds inside of you for your survival. Just keep showing up!

Be mindful of what you read.

Your emotions and mind are fragile after a significant loss. Some authors' messages gravitate toward their personal disbelief in faith, or they encourage you to lash out or sulk in your pain. Take precautions in the time after your loss to safeguard your heart and mind from content that doesn't speak the truth. This may look like self-help books that aren't rooted in Scripture.

Or it may include online influencers who tell you that you can do the work of true health and healing all on your own rather than reminding us that the work has already been done for us on the cross.

If you find yourself here, abandon the book, podcast, or article and just pray. Pray for them, pray for yourself, and pray for anyone who finds themselves lost in someone else's anger.

Find comfort knowing your baby is in Heaven.

Please rest assured that your baby is in Heaven. In Jeremiah 1:5, God tells Jeremiah, "Before I formed you in the womb I knew you, and before you were born I consecrated you." These words assure us that God is the Creator of life at conception. They also tell us that while Jeremiah was still in the womb, God was working through him.

You see, it doesn't matter at what point after conception your baby left this Earth. God distinguishes in this verse that there is no difference between life inside the womb or after birth. He reminds us also that His Holy Spirit resides in the womb in the account of Elizabeth's visit to Mary in Luke 1:

> *In those days Mary arose and went with haste into the hill country, to a town in Judah, and she entered the house of Zechariah and greeted Elizabeth. And when Elizabeth heard the greeting of Mary, the baby leaped in her womb. And Elizabeth was filled with the Holy Spirit, and she exclaimed with a loud cry, "Blessed are you among women, and blessed is the fruit of your womb! And why is this granted to me that the mother of my Lord should come to me? For behold, when the sound of your greeting came to my ears, the baby in my womb leaped for joy. And blessed is she who believed there would be fulfillment of what was spoken to her from the Lord.*

It was said that Elizabeth was around six months pregnant at the time of this visit, and while unclear, it is believed that Mary had recently conceived and was in her first trimester. The significance of this moment lies in the fact that John, being six months in utero, recognized the presence of his Lord, Jesus Christ, who was also in utero. This is evidence that the Holy Spirit resides in the womb. It is also proof that the Holy Spirit was with your baby from the moment of conception to the moment his or her heart stopped beating, and he or she is now united with Jesus in Heaven.

Our babies were never alone! And you are not alone in your grief for your baby. For just as you loved your baby deeply, so does our Lord. He resided in the heart of your baby from the moment of conception, and He never left his or her side. What a glorious day it will be for all of us when we are reunited with both Jesus and our babies in Heaven!

Scripture Verses of Comfort

If you are stuck and cannot pray or do not know where to start in your faith journey, simply ask the Lord for help. He will hear you, and as you open your heart to Him, He will help you.

The following passages offer encouragement, consistency, and the promise that you are not alone.

Isaiah 41:10: "Fear not, for I am with you; be not dismayed, for I am your God; I will strengthen you, I will help you, I will uphold you with my righteous right hand."

Psalm 34:18–19: "The Lord is near to the brokenhearted and saves the crushed in spirit. Many are the afflictions of the righteous, but the Lord delivers him out of them all."

Psalm 34:17: "When the righteous cry for help, the Lord hears and delivers them out of all their troubles."

1 Corinthians 10:13: "No temptation has overtaken you that is not common to man. God is faithful, and He will not let you be tempted beyond your ability, but with the temptation, He will also provide the way of escape."

James 4:8: "Draw near to God, and He will draw near to you."

John 3:16: "For God so loved the world, that He gave his only son, that whoever believes in Him should not perish but have eternal life."

Psalm 27:13–14: "I am still confident of this: I will see the goodness of the Lord in the land of the living. Wait for the Lord, be strong and take heart and wait for the Lord."

Psalm 22:10: "From birth I was cast upon you, from my mother's womb you have been my God."

Philippians 4:7: "And the peace that surpasses all comprehension will guard your hearts and your minds in Christ Jesus."

Miscarriage Prayer

My Lord, the baby is dead!

Why, my Lord—dare I ask why? It will not hear the whisper of the wind or see the beauty of its parents' face—it will not see the beauty of Your creation or the flame of a sunrise. Why, my Lord?

"Why, My child—do you ask 'why?' Well, I will tell you why."

You see, the child lives. Instead of the wind, he hears the sound of angels singing before My throne. Instead of the beauty that passes, he sees everlasting Beauty—he sees My face. He was created and lived a short time so the image of his parents imprinted on his face may stand before Me as their personal intercessor. He knows secrets of Heaven unknown to men on Earth. He laughs with a special joy that only the innocent possess. My ways are not the way of man. I create for My Kingdom and each creature fills a place in that Kingdom that could not be filled by another. He was created for My joy and his parents' merits. He has never seen pain or sin. He has never felt hunger or pain. I breathed a soul into a seed, made it grow, and called it forth."

I am humbled before you, my Lord, for questioning Your wisdom, goodness, and love. I speak as a fool—forgive me. I acknowledge Your sovereign rights over life and death. I thank You for the life that began for so short a time to enjoy so long an Eternity.

—Mother M. Angelica

RECAP

Surviving When Your Faith Seems to Be Failing

Grace is a powerful thing to give yourself. Give yourself grace. Give yourself time for prayer. Give in to your doubts and immerse yourself in healthy words that breathe life into the dark hole you now have. Surrender yourself to the One who will give you all of this: Jesus.

- Find a spiritual companion.

- Gravitate toward burden bearers.

- Make time for prayer.

- Pick up or start a spiritual discipline.

- If you attend church regularly, do not stop.

- Be mindful of what you read.

- Find comfort knowing your baby is in Heaven.

Surviving People

Lord, I pray for all those people who have reached out to us with love and support. I pray for them as they grieve for us. I pray you will give them strength and encouragement through this. What a blessed thing—to have family and friends of faith.

—Janelle's journal entry, August 23, 2014

EARLIER, WE MENTIONED the importance of bold, brave friends. Friends who speak life into you and challenge you to do hard things. The ones who show up and keep showing up. The bold friends who help you grow and change. Those brave people who see your potential and change your path. Those are the people you need to gravitate toward, especially during your grief. During that deep season of grief, when your heart is broken and you are just trying to survive. When you'd rather just lay in bed, your eyes heavy with tears, or when you just want to quit and give up on life completely, you need those brave people. Those thoughts happened to Janelle—thoughts of *I can't do this* or *This is too hard to live with*—and the tears were too heavy. When you feel like going forward is too painful and you feel like you can't see the light at the end of the tunnel, you need those brave kinds of people.

Bold, brave friends are the ones who don't shy away from your mood changes. They don't act awkward or stay silent. The people you need now are the ones who are not afraid to say your child's name. The people who will just show up at your door and listen to you beg for help or be comfortable with your tears. They even let you speak hate about life. They may not have any words to make your loss better, but they are the ones in tune to what you need. Most moments, you may not even know what you need, but you do need these kinds of people. They might be burden bearers as previously mentioned, or simply trusted neighbors and friends.

Kelvi shares that she was humbled by the acts of kindness she received shortly after her loss. Friends, neighbors, and even people she barely knew were sending cards and mementos, showing up with meals, or sending flowers. Many of her church family members showed up too. One particular act of kindness that sticks out involves an older man that she attended church and Sunday school with regularly. This gentleman was skilled in leatherwork, and he crafted a handmade leather purse for her in sympathy for her loss. She recalls, "He stood at my front door holding the purse and offered such a kind message of sympathy to me. He said he likes to craft beautiful things for people experiencing hard times. I treasure that purse to this day."

Laurel remembered that some of the most compassionate acts of kindness she received came from the least expected people in town. "One day, an older gentleman gave me his condolences and then teared up as he told me about how he and his wife were never able to have children of their own until they were able to adopt over fifty years ago. Another day, a big, burly man who was a large animal client gave me the biggest and most genuine bear hug and briefly cried with me before we started fertility testing his bulls for the spring. Wonderful people would just step out of the woodwork when I needed it the most and expected it the least. They would do things such as buying my chicken wrap for lunch when I went up to the register to pay or giving me a beautiful, handmade quilt in memory of my son when my first daughter was born. I will never forget their selfless acts of kindness." It didn't matter what it was; the kindness of others spoke volumes to Laurel's heart.

ALL OTHER PEOPLE, though, you need to set boundaries with! Boundaries are not comfortable, but they are necessary. They give you and others parameters to work within. They are a healthy way for you to say no. Boundaries are the bumpers in a bowling lane that keep you on track when you can't control your emotions or the emotions of others. Boundaries, like bumpers, keep you from rolling into the gutter and help you stay on course, especially since your emotions are likely tender and easily affected.

Laurel recalls struggling with how to handle other people's problems. Gossip and petty complaints were especially hard for her to handle. In her view, those small problems seemed insignificant compared to her losing a child. She found this change in her was hard. All three of us found it extremely difficult to face the changes in ourselves, and trying to survive those changes often didn't seem possible.

Please know your emotions are as unique as your journey. No one's emotions come out in the exact same way or at the exact same time. We all have feelings, and all of your feelings are valid. People are going to process and manage their feelings differently than you. It's better and easier for you to recognize that difference rather than trying to figure out why someone is reacting or not reacting in the same way as you.

Janelle recalled her husband, Kirk, only having cried once during their time in the hospital during Eli's delivery. And when he returned home, he went back to work that next week. He did spend his time creating and carving memorial pieces in Eli's honor, but his emotions and Janelle's emotions were very different and affected their day-to-day activities differently.

Laurel also remembered a similar situation with her husband, Bryce. He seemed very somber and quiet for a few months, and he said that once he'd cried it out good in the truck while driving around, he was ready to embrace their loss and try to keep moving on. Laurel kept listening to Christmas music for as long as she could because hearing about the birth of Christ through music was soothing to her, while Bryce went back to listening to his hard rock music once again. People who go through the same situation can process things differently for different amounts of time, and again, that's okay.

Not only will men process the loss of your baby differently, but so will family and friends. God created each of us differently, and our individual life experiences have shaped each of us into who we are; nobody, not even a family member, will process this exactly like you do. And it is okay that they don't. (Notice we didn't say it is *easy* if they don't—but it is okay.) Try not to resent their way of processing the loss. Find ways to honor your feelings and emotions. Find special tributes or ways to incorporate your grief into every day or even into special holidays and events. Allow yourself to grieve in your own time and don't compare your own grief process to anyone else's. Being resentful of "petty" issues and realizing your emotions aren't being recognized or validated by others can turn your grief into hate and hurt. So it helps to be proactive in identifying triggers, whether that is people or places or things. Prepare yourself beforehand if you can.

While navigating other people's reactions to your loss, be prepared to be caught off guard emotionally by how your loved ones are trying to process it. As much as parents grieve for lost babies, so do siblings. Kelvi's journal entry four months after her loss stated: "Kacy asked me, 'Why did our baby have to die?' That bothered me all night." "Kacy was only four years old at that time and was at the age of 'everything babies,'" Kelvi explained. "We took her baby doll in a car seat with us, she played with several at a time, and she even had her own 'daycare.' She was greatly looking forward to being a big sister." Even now, when Kelvi remembers feeling sad for Kacy, pangs of guilt set back in. We encourage you to not hide your emotions from your other children. Instead, show them healthy habits of talking through emotions when they come up, not suppressing them. Allow your other children to grieve with you and not alone.

I don't really understand the depth of Heaven and all of Jesus's love, but I do trust they are both real.

In Janelle's journal, she wrote this:

"I loved listening to the girls talk about Eli today. They shared how Eli was having 'boy time' with God. They were curious as to what Eli and God would talk about during boy time. I told them that he must be listening to Jesus talking about us. I do hope that is true—that Jesus is comforting my little guy with stories about who we are and how much we love him. I don't really understand the depth of Heaven and all of Jesus's love, but I do trust they are both real. I do trust there is 100 percent happiness and joy in Heaven and the people whom God made do go to Heaven, a place so glorious words cannot describe."

Hearing gentle words of remembrance from people can spark an onset of questions or even confusion for children. As much as it hurts, try to be present with them during this time. You may not have all of the answers, but just being there can ease their uncertainty.

Over the years, it has become easier for all of us to talk openly with our surviving children about their sibling in Heaven. By talking through the loss, it makes the sting less harsh when a sibling brings it up. Not only that, but by braving your feelings and making yourself vulnerable to talking through the pain with your children, you are teaching them two important lessons. First, it is both healthy and okay to talk about feelings of grief and sadness. Second, it is okay for them to see you cry and be sad. This is where we, as parents, can teach our children that we are all human and our emotions are nothing to be ashamed of. We do, however, need to show them that although we are sad, we can't stay there, and we have to support each other in taking the steps toward healing.

On this path of loss and grief, the three of us can tell you that you will be changed. Changed by the immense feelings you have for the baby you lost. Changed by the hurt for those future plans that died right alongside your child. And you will be changed by people. For us, this change was not gradual—it came quickly and without warning. It was, in part, a death for our old selves. We all noticed that part of us died with our babies.

Janelle still grieves about losing the person she was before. Her fast-paced, never-say-no, "I can do that and that and that and that" attitude was gone. And she had changed. "There was this new sense of slowness. A reality of the outcome of life. My view of success changed, and I didn't care about what was once important to me. At times, I recognized a feeling of contentment where I wasn't wanting more in life. I felt aged."

And with that change, you could possibly feel that change reflected in your relationships with any children you already have or have subsequently. It can be hard to connect to them and want to be close to them right after your loss. It's hard to have patience with them and their trivial needs. You may find yourself getting angry quickly or becoming disengaged with their daily routines. Their needs and wants can trigger more pain and sadness. You may not feel like you can face them or tolerate them. If this happens, you may encounter guilt because you feel like you should be able to love them like you did before. But again, we believe loss changes you.

You are no longer the same person you were before. We understand feeling scared about not being who you were before. But a diamond doesn't become a gemstone unless it's undergone extreme pressure and change. And you are a diamond. You *can* stand the pressure. God changed the hearts of so many people. He changed the course of our lives, and He is changing yours too.

These changes will affect the people around you. Besides your spouse and any children you already have, there will be people outside your family who will react to you and your grief in different ways. Some will throw their support and comfort to you weekly, monthly, and even yearly, on the anniversary of your loss. Other people will hold on to their patience and understanding of your pain and dissociations for a few months, but then they'll expect you to move on. You may face people who won't even acknowledge you had a loss, people you know who simply stare at you while you're out grocery shopping. You may find people you need to set the firmest boundaries with early on your journey. There will be all types of "those" people. Set boundaries.

Don't worry about making people feel uncomfortable. If you need to talk about your sweet baby, then please do it.

Laurel shared that going to the store after her loss was hard for her. Losing Forrest was so debilitating that when she went out in public, she felt like the spotlight was on her and everyone was judging her, even perfect strangers—like they knew her "secret." All those people, though, didn't even know who she was and didn't know what she was going through. For Laurel, people who would kindly acknowledge her loss were more appreciated than those who were silent. Whether it was family or community members, the people who stayed silent or avoided the topic were not where she found help. She chose not to worry about them. She reiterated, "Don't worry about making people feel uncomfortable. If you need to talk about your sweet baby, then please do it."

You will find women, old and young, who have walked in your shoes. Their loss may be different than yours, but they understand what it's like to feel loss. These women may squeeze your hand in church, leave a carved stone on your baby's fresh, unmarked grave, bring a casserole to your door, or hand you a pink-and-blue pregnancy loss pin. You will build new relationships, so don't be afraid to let go of past relationships that no longer fill your cup.

Tips for Surviving People

Some of the hardest things that we encounter daily are the people who cross our path. They all have opinions, advice, comments—kind and ill-intentioned. But their interactions with us affect our journey, especially after loss. We've listed a set of tips for finding ways to survive your interactions with others. While we ultimately believe most people mean well, the way they behave and speak and how we receive those cues and comments can truly affect our emotions when struggling with child loss.

Don't take unintentionally hurtful words to heart.

You've gotta love people. Sometimes they genuinely have good intentions, but their words come out totally wrong. While some people may offer you advice that can help you heal, others will try to say what sounds good at the time but will only make you feel worse. These words and phrases can sting:

"You can always have another one."

"Something must have been wrong with the baby. This is God's way of taking care of it."

"Oh, a miscarriage. Yeah, I had one of those once."

These statements can come across as unsympathetic and harsh to the mom who just suffered a loss. For some moms, the thought of having another baby is too hurtful because all they can think about in the short term is the grief they are carrying for the baby they just lost. Perhaps you are struggling just to get through today, and when someone diminishes or does not validate how impactful this loss has been to you, you feel like they are completely out of touch. Don't take these statements to heart. Don't let them resonate in your soul. You know the statements that lift you up, so release those hurtful statements and focus on the ones that fill your soul.

Set good boundaries.

Establishing boundaries is hard. Deciding what is good to keep in and what is good to keep out can be difficult. However, in relation to surviving emotionally after a miscarriage, good boundaries are essential. It takes courage to pull back from something or someone who is robbing you of your peace or time. In a season of emotional fragility, we encourage you to set boundaries with anyone who does not aid in your healing. If you need more help learning strategies to set boundaries, we highly recommend the book *Boundaries.* In these pages, authors Dr. Henry Cloud and Dr. John Townsend teach you how to not only set boundaries but learn about living within the "freedom to walk as the loving, giving, fulfilled individual God created you to be."

Be prepared for the silence.

You are going to be surprised by who you think will reach out but doesn't; you'll also be surprised by who you would have never guessed would reach out but does. One of the most surprising things after a loss might not be the people who do come up to you, but instead it might be the people you expected to see or hear from who are silent. Going back to work and having a colleague or close coworker fail to acknowledge your loss can be extremely difficult. Some people do not know *how* to acknowledge your loss, and rather than be uncomfortable themselves, they choose silence. So be prepared.

Approach family members with grace.

When silence comes from family, it can feel especially painful. These are the people who shared your journey, your love for the one you lost—and when they don't acknowledge your grief, it can feel like abandonment. Sometimes that silence stems from their own fear of saying the wrong thing, but that doesn't make it hurt any less.

One of Kelvi's family members told her after her loss that they weren't sure if they should mention Karaline or if she'd rather they not talk about it. Don't put up a wall with them. Instead, approach the subject with grace. Tell them you want to talk about your loss with them. In short, tell family members what you need.

Give your spouse extra grace.

Men process things differently. You and your spouse are not on the same timeline. They do want to help you through your grief, but at times they may not know how. Don't be resentful toward them.

Keep communication lines open. It is hard to process these emotions, and it's even harder to communicate them to others. We encourage you to be open with your spouse and take the emotional journey with them rather than each of you taking it alone. If talking to them directly is uncomfortable, ask them to sit in with you while you talk to a counselor, or write your feelings down and share them. While there is individual growth through the grief process, there can also be growth together.

Cling to good friends and modify your relationships with bad ones.

Your loss is now a part of who you are. Some friends will like you better before your loss and won't want to acknowledge this big change in your life. If a friend can't love this part of you too, your relationship may shift from how it was before to something less personal, and that is okay! On the other hand, you may find new friends, and beautiful relationships may grow out of grief.

If you aren't feeling like you have a place at a table of old friends, don't continue to sit there. Create your own table.

If you feel unseen or unheard by your friends and are "sitting around the table" feeling like you no longer connect with acquaintances, be bold and reach out to new friends. Perhaps a mother who has had a loss similar to yours reached out to offer comfort during your grief. Maybe you run into someone at your kids' ball practice or classroom activities and you'd like to get to know them better. Go ahead and make the first move. Give them a call and see if they'd like to grab coffee or dinner.

YOUR "TABLE" is the people you choose to do life with. They are the people you let into your inner circle of thoughts and desires. They are the people you choose to sit down with, laugh with, and talk life with. The people you'd choose to share a meal with. The people who add to your life. We each build a table of people who meet us where we are in that particular season of life. Some people remain around your table and walk through this difficult season of shifting and change. While others will not be able to stay or will need to be asked to leave.

You are what you think and
you create what you need.

We cannot express this enough: You are what you think and you create what you need. So find for your "new" self a group of people who offer you grace, sympathy, forgiveness, and support, and create a group who will stick beside you through anything. Create a group who deserves to stay at your table.

RECAP

Surviving People

Surviving people around you will take work. It'll take grace and for-giveness. It'll take boundary setting and communication. You will need to navigate relationships gently as your perspective most likely has changed.

- Don't take unintentionally hurtful words to heart.

- Set good boundaries.

- Be prepared for the silence.

- Approach family members with grace.

- Give your spouse extra grace.

- Be present for your children and encourage communication.

- Cling to good friends and modify your relationship with bad ones.

Surviving Trigger Days, Milestones, Holidays, and the Grave

Life continues. The tears came during the "Happy Birthday" chorus because I will never get to sing to Eli. He will not ever know his sisters or celebrate their special days.

—Janelle's journal entry, month 2

Whatever this day may bring, Lord, let thy name be praised.

—Unknown author

AFTER YOU LOSE A CHILD, some days are just harder than others. Days when that punch in the gut knocks you down again and it feels like your loss was just yesterday. Days that swallow your current survival mode and make you feel like you're starting all over again on your path. Some days are just like that. They hurt! Those days can feel like a jagged rock you've been carrying in your pocket that has slowly been smoothed down over days of being held and carried; now it has been chipped again and is poking you, making your emotions resurface and become raw again.

Janelle understands this all too well. "In the beginning, I remember everything was a trigger. Morning sunrises were triggers because of the blue and pink colors that symbolize infant loss. I'd look off into the blue-pink sunrise sky and be reminded of the vast number of babies who are gone and I'd cry. I'd ask for peace and comfort. I'd stand outside listening to the birds and crying for my little Eli." Even looking at family photos was a trigger.

One particular photo hanging in Janelle's living room was a trigger—it was a photo in which her two daughters sat side by side with an unplanned empty place between them that would be forever empty. Eli was supposed to be a part of that photo shoot. Every time Janelle looked at that picture, she would be hit with a wave of tears and extreme sadness.

A huge milestone that took Laurel by surprise was when Forrest would have turned five years old and should have been starting kindergarten in the fall. Laurel's niece, Willa, was born in October 2018; her nephew, Jameson, was born in January 2019; and another niece, Faith, was born in May 2019. Forrest was delivered still in November 2018, though his due date was in February 2019. When Willa and Jameson started kindergarten in 2024, Laurel didn't think much about it. When Faith, the last of these four cousins born close together, started kindergarten two weeks later, Laurel lost it. Out of nowhere, she was overcome with waves of sadness, feelings of loss and grief, about the boy she didn't get to know or raise here on this Earth. Her sweet boy would have been five! He should have been starting kindergarten like his cousins. What would he have been like—kind and helpful, or ornery and smart? What kind of backpack would he have picked out for school? Would he have liked tractors or dinosaurs? The emotions welled up inside her and she couldn't help but cry right there at work. Just like that, something can come out of nowhere when you least expect it and set you back just when you thought you were starting to find your footing with your grief.

Halloween was the first holiday without Eli. "I honestly can't recall much of the day other than it was the first Halloween since I began teaching that I didn't dress up for the kids at school. I didn't want to participate. I didn't want to be festive. I was tired and sad and over all the small, seemingly insignificant components of life. I found myself frustrated with what everyone was complaining about because none of it really, truly mattered. I was hurting, and the idea of celebrating a holiday rushing around and smiling was more than I wanted to do. So holidays were hard."

Janelle goes on to share, "Christmas was another trigger for tears and sadness. I sat in church during the candlelight service and cried. I missed Eli. I had just rejoiced during the previous Christmas Eve service, secretly knowing I was pregnant, and now I had nothing. Our family still went to church. We still held on to traditions and showed up. But we needed to make new traditions too. We purchased what we call an "Eli Tree." It's a small, green pencil tree. We started by hanging up an ornament we received from a caring community member who wanted us to have something in

Kirk and Janelle's yearly Eli Tree

remembrance of Eli. Each year since, we have purchased a new ornament that matches what we think Eli might be interested in at the age he should be." Knowing yearly that we can draw on our loss and turn it into beauty helps us heal.

Mother's Day was Laurel's first hard holiday. At church that morning, the priest asked all the mothers to stand up to be honored and receive a special Mother's Day blessing. Laurel felt like a failure because she didn't have any physical children here with her on Earth, though she knew she had at least three babies up in Heaven. Laurel remained seated during the special blessing and tried to hold back her tears. Although the priest had good intentions for the blessing, she couldn't help but feel like she had been singled out. And what about other mothers who had lost their children, or mother figures who didn't have children of their own? She cried for all the women hurting in some way from a hole in their heart. She cried because even though she knew she had her own children, she felt like she had nothing to show for her most recent experience with pregnancy.

That first Mother's Day, Bryce surprised Laurel with a light blue decoration bike that held three flowerpots. He hugged her, saying she was the best bonus mom to his kids and to their babies in Heaven. She still cannot explain the feelings of validation she received when Bryce gave her that bike. She had been an emotional mess, missing her sweet Forrest and wondering what he would have been like, and that gift was just what she needed. Now when she decorates that bike every spring and puts flowers in the three pots, she cannot help but think about her three babies in Heaven who are watching out for their family.

Holidays and milestones after your loss will combine two big emotions at once: joy and grief. You will build up to the day with such great joy and anticipation, only to be let down once that day arrives because all you can feel is grief for what is missing. As time goes on, you will still feel both— sometimes simultaneously—but preparing yourself beforehand can help you get ahead of those emotions before they surface unexpectedly and overwhelm you.

Kelvi remembers, "One of the hardest holidays for me to navigate after my miscarriage was Mother's Day. My first Mother's Day after my loss came five short months after we buried Karaline. I was stressed out and anxious during the weeks approaching, and little did I know I would be taken by complete surprise by the combustion of emotions bursting to the surface. I had not prepared myself mentally for the day. Quite honestly, I didn't think it would be much different than any other Mother's Day.

"I awoke that Sunday morning to beautiful cards from both Karlton and the girls, and we stuck to our normal tradition of attending church and doing "whatever Mom feels like doing" for our afternoon plans. Our church does a wonderful job of honoring mothers on that day. Children sing at the front, and the preschool class hand-delivers homemade cards afterward. As I sat in the pew watching my three girls sing, the lump in my throat and the ball of anxiety inside me grew. I was completely surprised by how fast and furious my emotions were coming on. I looked around the church to keep my eyes moving, blinking to hold back my tears. All I could think about was Karaline and how I should have been almost ready to deliver her. I sat stoic as the kids sang, thinking of everything else but the here and now. I felt like my emotions were boiling up inside my chest, and I was about ready to explode as I tried to stay present. I managed to survive the service without breaking down but wanted nothing more than to return home, crawl into my bed, and let the tears loose on my pillow.

"When I did return home, I did not want my grief to steal the day away from me, Karlton, and the girls, so I prayed for relief and something to make me feel better. That's when I remembered some advice I had received from my Sister nun, Sister Esther, who I'd visited at the Dominican Sisters of Peace. She suggested that I write Karaline a letter, so that is exactly what I did."

My Dear Sweet Karaline,

I am so sad that you are not here with me on Mother's Day. I love you so much. I am so sorry you had to leave this Earth so soon. Mother's Day will never feel the same because as much joy that I get from your three sisters, I have an emptiness in me and a broken heart for you.

I long to hold you and often wonder what you would be like growing up. When I look at your sonogram picture, your profile looks like Kacy's. You have a sweet little nose like hers that is short and turns up at the end.

I am so sorry my body went into labor, but I know God has taken you home and you are safe there.

Your sisters would've all loved you so much, especially Kacy right now.

You would've had the best dad in the world here on Earth. I get so sad to think he will never get to walk you down the aisle.

I also get sad a lot in church when the kids sing because I know I will never get to see you do that.

I can't wait to see you in Heaven. I am going to squeeze you so tight in my arms you can't breathe.

Please know how much I love you. My heart hurts for you, but I know you are in a better place.

I love you—Mom

"I want to share how cathartic it was for me to write this letter. It was the psychological release of emotions written down on paper that allowed me to breathe again. My hope is that if you are feeling a combustion of emotions inside, you allow yourself to release them. Get it all down on paper. What you do with it afterward is up to you. Sister Esther had suggested

I could take the letter to the cemetery and read it to Karaline. After I was done writing, I did not have the energy left in me to do that, but I treasure this letter in its raw, emotional state."

JANELLE ALSO CHANNELED her pain into a letter for her baby. "Writing something to your baby allows the hurt to surface and can be a source of immense heartache and pain," shared Janelle, "but it offers benefits to the soul. These benefits may go unseen for a while, but even if you can't see the changes, you can begin to feel the small doses of hope rising to the surface of your words. Opening up and letting your emotions flow through a letter to your child can allow for deep, soul-healing help."

Janelle wrote this following section for Eli:

Little Eli,

My heart aches for you. My arms long to hold you. My mind is filled with thoughts of you. Oh how I wish I was as strong as you. How I wish I wasn't uncertain. You, my little guy, are a blessing. You are teaching me sacred life lessons. Thank you. Please feel my love for you. Feel how my heart beats for you. Know how I love you even in my anger, even in my selfish, desperate days, I love you. In my sadness, help me feel you and see you. I pray that I will honor you. That when people see me—they see you, and they see God. That I live with you every day, my sweet boy.

I am proud to be your mommy, Eli. So proud to have known your kicks and hiccups. So proud to have made a lifetime of memories with you and your sisters that summer. So proud that God had a plan and your life will live on through me. You are my greatest contribution to this world . . . you and your siblings.

Love, Mom

It's not always the holidays that will hurt your heart. It can be places that are special or even sacred to you. The grave marker can be a place you need to survive. If other people leave unexpected memorials or kind gestures, you may find yourself upset or even territorial. Janelle found that changes to Eli's gravesite were a trigger of frustration for her. When those happened, instead of feeling a sense of support, she had a strong need to protect the gravesite.

Laurel visits Forrest's grave every Sunday after church with her husband, Bryce. If they are out of town over the weekend or she cannot visit because she's working, Laurel frequents the grave at least once weekly, sometimes daily. She decorates for the seasons and holidays by changing out a wreath for Forrest. It is their place. A place that needs protection and care. It has become a routine part of Laurel's week to check on Forrest, her baby, to make sure everything is all right, cleaned up, and taken care of. It's her way of caring for her baby even though he's not here on Earth with her.

Tips for Surviving Trigger Days, Milestones, Holidays, and the Grave

Every day on the calendar can bring new and challenging elements to surviving your loss. While any day can be hard, some days just "hit" harder. It may be an anniversary day event, or an observed holiday in which gathered family stirs up loss or longing, but you will find days that are tough. You may even not recognize the significance of a day until you stop and think about the calendar and how that particular day fits into your loss journey. You may not even be aware that particular days affect you. But when you slow down and reflect, you may begin to see a pattern of hard days during a particular timespan or season. We have listed a few of the "hard" days that we encountered in our healing as well as how we handled those days.

Mentally prepare yourself for feeling emotional.

If this is a holiday, start thinking through the routine and how you are going to tackle it. Walk through all the different activities and plans for your day—the church service, the dinner afterward, opening presents—but be ready when you are surprised by your emotions, and have a plan to sift through them when they occur. For example, if you are attending church and the service typically includes a children's program, prepare yourself in advance for that portion of the service so it doesn't catch you off guard.

Change up traditions if necessary.

Holiday traditions can be stressful, and trying to tackle them while navigating loss can be daunting. Sometimes a distraction is welcome until the emotional trauma has had some time to settle and healing can begin.

For Kelvi, the first Christmas was overwhelming, and it was clear they needed to do something different. "Our first Christmas, two short weeks after losing Karaline, we opted to take the girls to an indoor waterpark and stay the night. We did not spend Christmas with family doing the normal activities." However, please don't stay in the mindset of avoidance. Learn to create healthy traditions, and be careful to not shut others out.

Extend an act of kindness on trigger days.

Performing an act of kindness on a trigger day can ease the sharpness of pain and allow some positivity and light to shine on a day that seems dark. The beginning of the school year is a trigger for Janelle. At the start of each school year, Janelle's in-laws choose to purchase a backpack, fill it full of school supplies, and have her donate it to another classroom/school.

Communicate your anxiety to others.

People do not know what you need unless you tell them. The key is communicating your emotions in kindness before they erupt in anger. Communicate your concern of being overwhelmed by emotion to your spouse or a close friend. Grab a trusted family member and take a short walk to allow yourself some breathing room during family get-togethers or events.

Commemorate milestones.

Due dates are hard. Delivery dates are hard. Others in your life will miss recognizing these days, and the more time that passes, the more often it will happen. So celebrate the baby you carried. Celebrate their memory in a way that honors them and your feelings. It can be big or it can be small.

On Karaline's Birthday, Kelvi's family buys a Dairy Queen ice cream cake, sings her happy birthday, and spends the time remembering the fourth girl of their family.

On Eli's Day, Janelle's family makes an angel food cake and takes a picnic lunch to nearby Mushroom Rock State Park. There they hike and eat and share intentional family time. They also take an updated family photo. Janelle takes the day off on Eli's Day and goes through sympathy cards, listens to music, opens his box of items from the hospital, and looks through photos. She visits the cemetery; she sits in the quiet of the day.

Laurel always felt bad about not doing "something special" on Forrest's Anniversary, such as baking him a cake or singing to him. On his first anniversary, however, she and Bryce talked about what they should do to honor him yearly and decided to keep it simple. On Forrest's Anniversary, Laurel's family visits him at his gravesite, and they talk about what a great big brother he would have been to his younger siblings.

There is no right or wrong way to honor your baby.

Write your baby a letter.

Write your feelings down on paper. Perhaps you'd like to read it aloud to your baby in Heaven, either at the cemetery or at home. Or perhaps you don't want anyone to read it after it is written. Whatever you choose to do with the letter is okay! If a milestone or holiday is causing you extra anxiety, this is a great way to release those tough emotions.

WHATEVER YOU CHOOSE TO DO, however you choose to honor your baby, there is no right or wrong way. And there is no right or wrong thing you can call the day you lost your baby, whether it's a birthday, their day, an anniversary, or something else. You just need to do what is best for you and your family and talk about it how you see fit.

RECAP

Surviving Trigger Days

Milestones, anniversary dates, and visiting the grave can cause immense emotional pain. We encourage you to lean into them rather than ignore them. As time goes on, the heaviness will lift, and your ability to maneuver emotional outbursts will become second nature.

- Mentally prepare yourself for feeling emotional.

- Think through the activities and plans for the day.

- Change up traditions if necessary.

- Extend an act of kindness on trigger days.

- Communicate your anxiety to your spouse, close friends, or family.

- Commemorate milestones.

- Write your baby a letter.

Surviving Infertility or a Subsequent Pregnancy

... and to think, the first thing you saw when you opened your little eyes was the face of Jesus.

—Laurel's "crutch" quote, author unknown

I sit here today holding on to the memory of Eli while also trying to be present in this moment. The moment of new possibilities, of new life. But all the while fearful that in just another single moment it could all be gone again.

—Janelle's journal entry

THERE'S FEAR ... AND THEN there's "pregnancy after loss" fear. A fear that debilitates you and keeps you from enjoying those flutter kicks and hiccups in utero. A fear that keeps you awake at night longing for one more kick just to make sure everything is okay. Pregnancy after loss is a whole different level of worry and stress. It's a whole bunch of "I wonder if everything is okay" and "I probably shouldn't plan on this working out" and maybe a few "I shouldn't bother getting my hopes up" comments. Maybe those remarks only swirl around in your head and never get uttered, but pregnancy after loss is hard. There is worry. There is doubt. There is uncertainty and distrust. Distrust of your body. Distrust of the process.

The grief you've experienced has cast this looming shadow over the process from conception to birth. And while there is joy coming—this distrust, this doubt, this cloud has made you question your body and soul's abilities. You are trying to trust but holding back. It's a roller coaster of excitement and anguish. A start–stop journey. It's 40 weeks of praying for the best while never fully believing it'll actually happen, and that wears down the heart. That cloud of doubt trying to break you and take away the joy of new promise—it's hard. It's stressful. It's a whole different level of fear. That's the fear that comes with subsequent pregnancies after a loss.

Laurel and Bryce have such a personal journey with this. While they do have a home with children, the babies they lost can't be overlooked or forgotten. That can often be the case for women who have suffered loss: They will have more children. But none of those babies were the ones they had lost. They don't take the place of or fill the holes left by the babies they didn't get to bring home. When your heart is ripped out and ripped open, all you want is *that* baby.

Laurel got pregnant one month after being married in 2017. They had their first miscarriage with that baby at nine weeks. They chose to try again. It took four months to conceive, and in November of 2018, at 28 weeks, Forrest was delivered still. In June 2019, they suffered a second miscarriage, this time at six weeks' gestation. Followed by nine long months of trying. Loss. Heartbreak. Pain. Yet through all this, they held faith.

Being labeled as having "infertility" issues was so hard for Laurel. Why could they get pregnant right away after getting married, but then it took longer and longer to get pregnant after each loss? Was something really wrong with her? To try to understand why it was taking longer each time to get pregnant, various tests and methods were used to rule out any medical issues. Complete blood work panels were run, reproductive tract imaging was performed, ovulation induction medications were used; even Bryce's health was evaluated. Was this all because of stress building up from not being able to get pregnant, being labeled as having "infertility issues," or knowing they were on a "time crunch" because Bryce was ten years older than her? Or were these longer gaps between pregnancies just Laurel's body telling her it needed some extra time to heal between losses?

Along her journey of infertility, Laurel found out that nothing is certain, and questions frequently remain unanswered. Similar to what she saw in her world as a veterinarian, even after her doctor ruled out possible problems or diseases, sometimes there just aren't clear answers. As per Laurel's OB-GYN, fertility is such a multifactorial issue that often there isn't just one reason patients find it difficult to get pregnant. Oftentimes a patient's diagnosis may be called "unexplained infertility." Thankfully, though, there are methods to assist patients in conceiving, such as ovulation induction medications, intrauterine insemination, and in vitro fertilization.

Laurel found that each time she finally became pregnant, there was so much joy along with grief, pain, and fear. It seemed like she was holding her breath until she would pass the 6 week pregnancy mark, the 9 week mark, the 28 week mark . . . and even then, she knew something could happen at any time. She was trying to protect her pregnancy—her baby—and at the same time hoping her body wouldn't betray her.

After losing Forrest and having two miscarriages, Laurel's subsequent pregnancies involved more frequent ultrasounds and fetal monitoring—anywhere from two to three weeks apart depending on her work schedule. According to her OB-GYN, there is a very old plan for patients with recurrent pregnancy loss called the "TLC" protocol. The original protocol called for weekly ultrasounds, and this more frequent monitoring showed a reduction in miscarriage from 51 percent down to 26 percent between the two groups. Doctors who use this protocol may modify it depending on each patient and their personal histories. Not only does this practice help make a difference in pregnancy outcomes; it also helps with patient reassurance, and that reassurance was what Laurel really needed.

To try and help ease her fears at home, Laurel also bought a fetal doppler. This allowed her to monitor the baby's heartbeat if she was having any doubt about how she was feeling or if something potentially compromising had happened at work. Hearing a baby's fetal heartbeat will still bring Laurel to tears because she knows just how precious that sound is, and that it should not be taken for granted. She still offers her thanks to God for each heartbeat she was able to hear with her pregnancies as all babies are such a miracle and blessing in themselves, no matter how short a time they may be with us.

Whether your journey with loss is less or so much, much more—whether you have lost one or ten babies or struggled with conceiving—we see you. We want to offer all our encouragement and love to you. We don't say we know exactly what you are experiencing, but we do recognize your suffering, and we want to encourage you in your walk. There can be redemption. Maybe not in the exact way you hope, but have heart—God is near. And He will raise you up in your pain.

For Janelle, the miscarriage she suffered between Eli and Callen's birth in 2017 helped her recognize what an immense internal battle it is for women who struggle with infertility. The growing frustration and hurt. The disappointment. She was overcome with the worry of not ever becoming pregnant again and the heartache of possibly losing another baby in utero. She not only questioned the call of being parents to another child, but she also questioned her strength to survive yet another possible loss.

In a sense, Janelle spent that season of loss hiding away. She was aware that first trimester miscarriages occur more frequently than second and third trimester miscarriages, which is why many people wait to share news of a pregnancy until after the twelve-week mark; for that very reason she didn't share much of her journey with others.

For Laurel, sweet Oaklynn was born in February 2021. She was followed by ornery Karter in September 2022. Her newest bundle of joy, Ledger, was born in May 2024. Yes, right in the midst of this book-writing journey. Joy in grief. Hurt while healing.

Laurel felt the same way that Janelle did about announcing her pregnancies too early. Since her first pregnancy ended in an early miscarriage, she was very wary of announcing her pregnancy with Forrest before twelve weeks. When they were finally ready—around 16 weeks—Laurel made a Facebook post about the newly expected addition to their family, complete with a photo of her and Bryce proudly holding up a onesie announcing the new baby coming in February 2019. After losing Forrest a few short months later, Laurel never posted any sort of baby announcement on Facebook again. She so wanted to shout her joy to everyone the moment she and Bryce found out about their subsequent pregnancies, but she was reserved, scared, and nervous to say anything, anticipating another loss at any time. Please know there is no right or wrong time to announce a pregnancy. If that is what you choose to do, you must do it in a way that makes you comfortable.

Feeling like you can't celebrate the potential birth of a new baby early on is frustrating. You're suffering from morning sickness, tiredness, hormonal changes, a possible wave of mental changes due to the pregnancy—and you feel pressure to do all of that privately. If you've been through loss already, you now have the intensified fear of losing another baby . . . combined with the intensified fear of having to go through a potential loss silently. You may also fear not having your loss acknowledged by others simply because it was an early-term loss. But you should not have to deal with these fears and feelings alone. Your table of people should be there to support you. No matter the stage or term length of pregnancy you are in, we want you to know you don't need to be silent.

Just like many people thought Eli was Janelle's only "real" loss because he was full-term, many people thought Forrest was Bryce and Laurel's only loss since he was further along at 28 weeks' gestation. Few people know of the two other miscarriages they suffered at 9 and 6 weeks' gestation, respectively. Some people have been known to "level" a miscarriage, insinuating that a baby who is lost later in gestation is more important than one lost earlier. A woman might lose a baby at 9 weeks, 16 weeks, 28 weeks, or full-term at 40 weeks. No baby is more important than another; they are all made equally in the eyes of God and are all called children of God.

And finally, there is the mother who longs for more children after her loss but never receives the gift of another pregnancy. For Kelvi, after losing Karaline and not having any children after her miscarriage, she always felt like something was unsettled or unfinished. Like her story of motherhood was cut off unnaturally and abruptly with no happy ending. She recalls comments of "at least you have three beautiful children already" and "be thankful for what you have." These comments seemed out of touch with her feelings of wanting the baby she lost and yearning to be pregnant again.

However you are feeling, we encourage you to speak about it to your burden bearer or counselor. Your feelings are valid and important to recognize. For Kelvi, peace over her entire journey came while navigating her deep, dark feelings of loss and shame with the support of both trusted burden bearers and professional counseling. If you are feeling unsettled, that same peace can and will come to you.

Tips for Surviving Infertility and Subsequent Pregnancy Stress

Just as your loss journey is uniquely yours, so is your fertility journey. The process of conceiving varies from woman to woman. And just as your process is uniquely yours, so is the process in which you manage infertility and subsequent pregnancies. We can only offer our perspective and encourage you to find a tip that helps you work through some of the stress that comes with this part of the journey. Please know that this is not a complete list. It is just a sample of strategies that can help you.

Talk about it and share your concerns with your spouse.

Janelle shared that she and Kirk had different viewpoints on trying to conceive again. She felt like they were intended to have more children, but Kirk was a bit more hesitant. He wasn't sure he could put himself through another August 21st. They ultimately decided to "let go and let God." If it was meant to be, then it would be. And eventually, God blessed them in the way of more children.

Get all of the information.

Ask your provider for a full evaluation and discuss potential prenatal care differences after fetal demise. From our experience, subsequent pregnancies after fetal demise pregnancies are more closely monitored. Our doctors requested weekly stress tests and ordered biweekly checkups after 32 weeks. Janelle's OB-GYN strongly encouraged scheduling an induction to be more planned during delivery. After the miscarriage she had following the stillbirth of Eli, setting an induction date made sense. Your best resource is your prenatal care physician, so listen to their guidance.

Ask the questions.

Don't feel guilty about "inconveniencing" a doctor or ultrasonographer by asking questions. If you want a little more time to hear that heartbeat or see the ultrasound, or if you want to run a different blood panel, ask. You may not get the answer you want, but at least you aren't walking out of the doctor's office still wondering.

Quit holding your breath for the next threshold.

Whether it's 9 weeks, 16 weeks, or 28 weeks, you have to surrender to the fact that you are not in control of your baby's life in the womb. Relax. Breathe. And trust that the same God who delivered you through the grief of your miscarriage will guide you and walk alongside you through the rest of your pregnancy or infertility journey.

Create your peace.

This is hard and will not come overnight. But our hope and prayer for you is that you do not live any longer in the worry, the unsettlement, or the unfinished part of your story. Choose to continue the journey with acceptance of what has happened in the past and the encouragement that your story is still being written.

WHILE WE CAN'T SPEAK TO many women's immense struggles of years' worth of infertility, the roller coaster of grief and joy with unsuccessful fertility drugs, or using surrogacy, we can share our little bits of truth when it comes to riding the overwhelming waves of worry and fear about losing another baby. We can share the steps we took with our practitioners during subsequent pregnancies. We can speak to you about the uncertain, uneasy, worrisome waves of emotions that spike when expecting again.

If you have experienced these emotions, know that the suggestions we offer throughout this book come out of love and encouragement for you. They come from our experiences, and we hope they will help you find reassurance in your journey. Having a baby after a loss can be challenging to maneuver through. Whether that be a child you call a rainbow baby or one you try not to connect to the loss of a baby before, be patient with yourself. Let go of the worry and hold on to hope.

RECAP

Surviving Infertility or a Subsequent Pregnancy

Having a baby after a loss or dealing with infertility can be challenging to maneuver through. Be patient with yourself. Let go of the worry and hold on to hope.

- Talk about it and share your concerns with your spouse.
- Get all of the information.
- Ask the questions.
- Quit holding your breath for the next threshold.
- Create your peace.

Surviving the Years to Come

The thought of another day without you just breaks me down—tears me up. You are supposed to be here. You're supposed to know my arms, my face, my love. I know God is greater and His love is greater, but it still hurts this momma. There are still incomplete dreams and missed chances. Eli—I love you. I loved you before I saw you. I loved you before I knew you could be. People love you, little one. You are a fan favorite.

You had so many admirers without them setting eyes on your cute face.

May there always be admirers. May they always remember you.

May this story be remembered and shared for you!

—Janelle's journal entry, week 3

THERE IS THIS OLD ADAGE: "Time flies when you're having fun." While that can be true, it can also be true to just say, "Time flies." And just like that, time can fly by so quickly!

Those first nights after losing Eli, Janelle said she could vaguely remember not wanting to close her eyes. Not wanting to sleep away his memory. Not wanting days to go by so she wouldn't have to move on from him and the brief time they shared. She remembered not really wanting time to pass at all. She wanted to never move on from that moment. Janelle worried that if she slept, she would somehow forget or she'd be further away from him; but all the while she was actually begging for sleep to take her. She was begging for days to move faster so she could be further from the pain. She wanted to be further down the road of loss so that it didn't consume her. Both at once. "Ten years later," Janelle said, "I'm wondering where the time went. Wondering how I got to this place. How in the world have I been able to move forward even in such a great loss?" Time keeps moving, whether we want it to or not. It marches forward steadily, whether or not we are having fun. Time just flies. It's partly survival—surviving the new.

Laurel often repeats another adage: "The days are long but the years are short." Six years out from losing Forrest, after adding three beautiful children to her family, she can also see that time is flying by. And she is healing. But it's not the time that is healing her wounds; it is all the work she is putting into her journey of grief.

On a snowy day in February 2025, Laurel dug through her closet at home to find her box of keepsakes from when she lost her sweet baby boy. At one point, she had put these painful memories away; she couldn't even really remember where she'd placed them. But after finding them buried deep in her closet with her wedding mementos, Laurel carried the purple bifold box tied with a ribbon and a pile of cards to the kitchen table.

As she sifted through the items in the box for the first time since she put them away years ago, she felt a sense of peace and heartfelt gratitude wash over her. She was reminded of the wonderful support system she had behind her, even though she felt at the time like she had been walking her path alone: people from church, ladies' golf league friends, vet school and high school friends, family, and coworkers. She held the small, crocheted hospital cap made for her baby, tearing up as she read the kind words and prayers people had written to her. Within the purple box, she found a set of clay handprints from Forrest, prayer cards, a CD containing images from the photographer in the hospital, hospital bracelets, a crucifix from Forrest's funeral, memorial money in an envelope, a dragonfly figurine, and the second braid from Bryce's long beard. So many good things to remember her sweet baby boy.

As she was slowly cherishing these memorial items, Laurel's four-year-old daughter, Oaklynn, had joined her at the table to see what she was doing. They were sitting next to a big picture window facing west overlooking a pear tree full of bird feeders. As Laurel was tearing up from reading one of the cards, Oaklynn shouted, "Look, Mommy, a red bird!" As Laurel blinked through her tears, sure enough, there was a cardinal sitting in the tree—a beautiful, red contrast to the soft, white snow around it. For Laurel,

*Laurel's thoughtful gift to Kelvi on the
fifth anniversary of losing Karaline*

cardinals had always been a symbol of someone from Heaven being near, and just like that, the cardinal was a reminder of Forrest's presence during that moment. Again, Laurel felt peace and reassurance that her sweet baby was in Heaven watching out for them.

Kelvi experienced a similar moment of peace. "Five years after the loss of Karaline, on December 12, 2023, I heard a knock at the door. Karlton or one of the girls answered it, and I rounded the corner from the other room to see Laurel standing in my foyer. She was holding a bag and a card. I opened it to see a beautiful statue of a hand holding a sleeping baby. Tears began to streak down both of our faces. 'I just wanted to let you know I'm thinking about you and your family, and I don't want your little girl to be forgotten,' she said to me. *Wow! What a touching moment,* I thought to myself. *How thoughtful that she remembered my sweet Karaline five years later and took the time to visit me.*"

The statue sits in her house as a reminder of not only Karaline but also the bravery and strength of Laurel continuing to show up for others. Even if you don't have a Janelle or Laurel to remember your baby, perhaps you can be that someone for the next mother on this path of loss. It may be a tool to help both of you continue healing.

You may be at the very beginning of this journey. You may be at a stage where you can't even imagine being two years, five years, or ten years out from your loss, and that's okay. Don't imagine that yet. Just be in the moment. Stay on your path. Acknowledge your feelings, find a survival tip to help you in that moment, and get yourself to tomorrow.

Tips for Surviving the Years to Come

You might be looking at this section of the book thinking, *I'm never going to get there*. But please trust us when we say that you can. You can get here. Step by step. Day by day. You can get to the Years to Come. The tips we've collected in this section can help you in the months and years ahead. One of the greatest gifts you can give your baby now is your survival story. Use these tips and work on your own list of beneficial tips to surviving.

Don't let others tell you what you should be doing or how you should behave. Honor your feelings and take the next step.

Don't let anyone influence your decisions in the "right after."

Do what *you* want and grieve how *you* want. Each of us can only encourage you to do what seems fitting for you in your deep grief. If you want to allow family members to meet your baby and hold them, then do that. If you want photos, take them. If you want to have a private burial, then do just that.

The day of, the day after, and the next few days will be hard, so don't let others tell you what you should be doing or how you should behave. Honor your feelings and take the next step.

Mentally prepare for the unexpected.

You will experience a lot of firsts that will catch you off guard when you decide to step out or even try to return to a normal routine. While we cannot predict them all, there are a few common situations that can be triggering to raw emotions after a miscarriage. These include but are not limited to:

- Seeing or holding a newborn for the first time
- Hearing the name of the baby you lost
- Seeing another pregnant woman at the grocery store

First and foremost, we want you to remember that it is okay and normal for you to feel these sudden pangs of sadness or anger. We are here to tell you, though, that this isn't a place to get comfortable in. By acknowledging ahead of time that these emotions are normal at first, you can start to take small steps to work through them.

Raw emotions can be initially overpowering. Remember to take deep breaths and speak positivity and grace to yourself. Be brave and bold enough to face these situations head on and not avoid them. You will find that with time, it will become easier to hold a baby, congratulate the next expectant mother, or even speak your baby's name.

Talk about grief and loss when you feel it come up.

Just because five years has passed doesn't mean your love for your baby has lessened. Over time, you will begin to notice that the more you talk about your loss, the better you will feel, the lighter your load may become, and the easier it will be to talk about when waves of emotions flood you.

Create something beautiful out of your grief.

We aren't saying you need to write a book or start the next big charity. We are simply encouraging you to turn your grief into joy by using the tough times as an opportunity to honor your love for your baby in a positive way. Refocus those ugly feelings of guilt, depression, shame, and sadness into ways to help others. Doing an act of honor—whether it's for your baby or someone else's—can create beauty and healing.

- Check in on an elderly neighbor or visit with someone who might seem lonely.
- Volunteer at a local food bank or homeless shelter.
- Check in on another mother who has experienced a loss.
- Create something. Build something. Channel goodness into your days. That is a way to find and share joy.
- Wear or display a memento of your baby as a reminder of how far you've come. It can be a reminder that although there is grief, there can be joy.

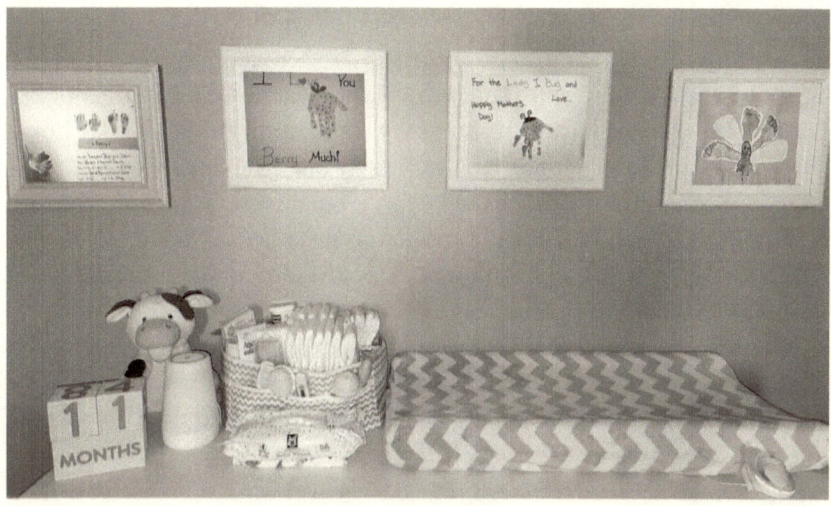

Forrest's handprints and footprints, hung next to his younger siblings' artwork

Kelvi wears a simple ring every day inscribed with the name "Karaline."

Janelle had a custom iron piece made by a local blacksmith. It's an outline of a butterfly, and it hangs on the wall between her second and third children's portraits.

Laurel framed and hung Forrest's handprints and footprints from the hospital. This frame is lined up on the wall with three other picture frames that hold her three other children's artwork.

One year out—Review your goals and keep going.

Being a parent of a child who is no longer living is one of the hardest things to do. On your first anniversary of your loss, plan something for your baby. Take the day off and go through your memory box or just take an extra-long walk. Spend the day in a way that lifts your soul and allows you to connect to this special baby.

We've mentioned it before and we'll do it again here: Your survival depends on you and what you put into your self-care and your health. It depends on your ability to find what soothes your pain. Each year to come will be a milestone, and it's important to mark those milestones with a planned purpose for you, your healing, and your baby.

Review the goals you have set for yourself—those daily goals you chose to help get you out of bed on those really hard days. Remove from that list what you are now able to do without too much effort. Now, pick a new goal or two for the new year. Janelle chose to start her second year without Eli as a "walking for life" year. She set the goal of walking daily in memory of Eli. She chose to walk to the cemetery, turn around, and walk back home every day—partly to get healthy, but partly as a conscious reminder that she could enter into the depths of her grief but choose to turn around and return into life. A life with the people who need her on Earth. A life that has joy and sorrow. A life that requires her to be intentional. So review your goals and make adjustments.

Continue to write out your three daily blessings. Three things that you choose to be thankful for each day. If you need some inspiration, you might even ask a family member to text you every day with their own list of three blessings, or at least a weekly recap of where they found joy that week.

Take time to evaluate where you've been and what things have helped you move forward, and keep some of these intentional habits going as you step into the years to come. Maybe you and your family decide to make financial donations to a charity in memory of your lost child or you find a meaningful way to contribute to others' losses. Whatever it is, focus on habits that bring healing and builds positivity in the year to come.

Five years out—Continue the remembrance.

Five years can seem to pass quickly. This threshold can be a point of reflection on how you have managed to work through the loss both mentally and physically. It is a reminder that perhaps you didn't do everything "right" or the way you wish you would've, but that's okay. You can pick up from here and keep moving in a healthy direction. Five years can allow wounds to heal and emotions to soften, giving you an opportunity to remind yourself how strong and resilient you are.

As Laurel reflected on the first five years after losing Forrest, she recognized the amount of growth she had undergone during that time—overcoming the darkest of days and coming out ahead of severe grief and depression. While every day was different and she still had setbacks along the way, she focused on finding joy in the grief and trying to make something good out of the bad. To continue growing in the future, Laurel has contemplated going to a counselor to talk about some anger that is starting to well up inside her. She would also like to write a letter to Forrest to help offer her some consolation and to keep guiding her down a path of healing.

If you have not chosen to recognize your loss in the prior four years but your heart is aching now at year five, we encourage you to find something to share with your baby this year. If you can't think of an activity, pick one that we've mentioned in this book and do that for your child.

Maybe this is the year your family wants to donate to a local church or community group in honor of your baby. Memorial moneys had been given in honor of Eli, and Janelle's church family used that to purchase and install a projector and screen for their Friendship Hall youth gatherings and presentations. Janelle shared that it wasn't in the first years after losing Eli that she was able to think about the memorial money and how it should be used. But in time, the church's idea of a screen and projector just felt right.

Finding what is right isn't easy, even in year five, but take the time to do something special, and take time to remember. Maybe all you want to do is buy yourself some fresh flowers. Then go and do that. Choose something that helps your heart.

Ten years out—Reflect on how brave you are and how far you've come

Janelle writes on her Facebook page each year on August 21st. On her ten-year mark, she wrote:

10 years. A decade.

Our days have turned into months and now our months have turned into years. 10 years to be exact. 10 years without Eli. These last 10 years have been both easy and hard. Full of blessings and sorrows. Full of despair and joy. They have brought comfort and hope, sadness and strength. They have brought new friendships and a new level of community. These past 10 years have been full of learning and navigating. Trying and failing. Walking forward in faith. They have been 10 years of memories and remembrance. Remaking and rebuilding. 10 years of walking this journey of grief and joy. They have been full of the same joy that surrounds us today as we think about our sweet baby—Eli. Each year has brought us a chance to find God's mercies and grace. To find His love and comfort. We have so much to be thankful for even on days like today. 10 years missing. A decade gone.

Continuing to write about her love and loss has helped Janelle in her healing.

You may find yourself in that same position: still doing some of the same things you did in the "right after" years later. Some of these patterns may be refined or modified, but you may keep them going because they make you better. They add to your life.

You are a brave woman.

At ten years out, you may find yourself in a completely different place than you ever imagined. And that in itself is amazing. You have done something that started out as unimaginable in the days "right after," and you should be proud of that. Not because the journey is done, but because you are still showing up every day.

You are a brave woman. You are that brave friend who is challenging yourself and others—because whether you know it or not, you *are* challenging others to keep going. And we are so proud of you.

RECAP

Surviving the Years to Come

You may be at the very beginning of this journey. You may be at a stage where you can't even imagine being two years, five years, or ten years out from your loss, and that's okay. Don't imagine that yet. Just be in the moment. Stay on your path. Acknowledge your feelings in that moment, find a survival tip to help you through it, and get yourself to tomorrow.

- Don't let anyone influence your decisions in the "right after."

- Talk about grief and loss when you feel it come up.

- Create something beautiful out of your grief.

- One year out—Review your goals and keep going.

- Five years out—Continue the remembrance.

- Ten years out—Reflect on how brave you are and how far you've come.

Surviving Your Role as a Support System

SOMETIMES IT CAN BE TOO OVERWHELMING to explain exactly what you need from those around you. You may not have the right words or the verbal strength to say what you want or what you need. You may not even know exactly what it is that you need. We understand that. If you find that you are struggling with articulating your needs, share this portion of the book with your support system. Share it with your people, your burden bearers, your colleagues, your family—if you are struggling to explain how they can support you and help you in your grief, then let this section speak for you. You can give your support people an opportunity to receive survival tips without having to come up with the words on your own. Asking for help and seeking help can take extra effort, and when your brain is working through grief, it can be much more difficult to explain what you need. So extend this section of the book to them.

You may be the only part of the journey that makes any sense. So be there for them. Love them. They need you.

Dear Family and Friends,

Welcome. You are an essential element in the survival story of a mother of loss. Your role and involvement in this journey are key. They need you. WE need you.

Through the hard days, the ugly days, the days full of tears, and yes even on the days that joy starts to shine through. Your words of encouragement will open their hearts to a new level of strength they never knew they had. Your role is vital. Do not shy away from their pain. Be gracious when they lash out. Be forgiving when they fail you. Offer them a shoulder to cry on, a hand up, or even a loving nudge.

We cannot say it enough: Be there. Be open. Say their child's name. Follow the lead of the one grieving. You may be the only part of the journey that makes any sense. So be there for them. Love them.

They need you.

Helping those suffering through a loss can be a difficult process to navigate for friends, coworkers, parents, and siblings. Seeing your loved one in pain and struggling with grief is difficult, and not knowing how to help them can add to the difficulty. What you say or don't say in the days, weeks, and months following a loss can greatly impact a person's ability to cope with a miscarriage or stillbirth. Helping your loved one heal begins with recognizing the loss itself—not by ignoring, dismissing, or downplaying it.

You, as a supporter, partner, family member, or friend, play a vital role. You are the first tier of support. You have firsthand knowledge of and an upfront seat to how grief is affecting your loved one. A grieving person may put on a face or not be fully open and honest with the world around them. But as a close friend or family member, you see that person when they take off their mask and really expose their hurt.

Your role in helping them survive may be more intense than you want or need to deal with. The person who has just lost so much may lash out at you or tell you really hard or dangerous things. You need to be a rational, wise, balancing sounding board for them. And that is a huge weight to carry. Don't look at it as a burden but see it as a gift—a chance to get an inner look into the life of someone who needs you. Because that's what grief needs: others.

Tips for Helping Others Through Their Grief

We've provided a set of tips and suggestions to help you help others through their loss and grief. You will find ideas that we've experienced through our losses that may assist a family member or friend who is struggling to share sympathies or express care. These tips are intended for your role as the support system.

Don't minimize the loss.

Saying things like "You can always have more" or "I had one of those too" can make the person feel like their feelings have no merit. Well-intentioned comments like this don't always sit well when grief and emotions are high. If you aren't sure what to say or what will be received, try saying, "I am just so sorry for your loss."

Follow the cues of the grieving family. If you are trying to decide if you should say something, the answer is simple: you should. You will never have the perfect words or the perfect thing to say to take away the pain, but the key is trying. The survivor will recognize your effort of compassion and sympathy and may open the door for you to come in, sit down, and talk for a while. If it is uncomfortable, try to set that feeling aside and just be present for the survivor. Sometimes your presence is enough.

Don't stay silent.

If you feel you don't know the right words to say, and you choose to say nothing at all, that can be even more hurtful to the survivor than something that doesn't roll off the tongue just right. For the person walking in grief, just hearing that other people acknowledge their pain is enough.

Not all people feel comfortable addressing emotional pain and hurt. Some people have never experienced intense grief. Not all people are talkers. Janelle's husband is that type of person. So recognizing his silence as part of who he is as a person, and not a symbol of his lack of care, was a key to Janelle not being disappointed or frustrated with the way he was coping. Try recognizing those "silent type" people and be aware that this is how they cope.

If you are a spouse, be patient with your partner.

You will not grieve in the same way or on the same timeline as your spouse, so try to recognize signs of struggle in your spouse. Be in tune with each other.

Check in on your loved one several times during their first few days back to work. Send a simple text to ask how they are doing. Calling over your lunch break is a great expression of care.

If they are having a bad day or a few bad days in a row, try to do something with your spouse; take them on a drive in the country, take them to a movie or dinner, go on a walk together, or start a Netflix series together. Be prepared for a negative reaction, but don't let your partner suffer alone. Being helpful around the house can also show your spouse that you acknowledge their pain. Try not to overthink it. Make a pot of coffee in the morning, start a load of laundry, load the dishwasher, or fill the car up with gas.

Janelle looked back through her journals and found an entry about how her husband, Kirk, took her on a weekend "get out" to a hotel. They could shut the curtains and just be in the quiet together. It made a huge impact on their togetherness as a couple. It was her husband's way to eliminate the visual reminders of the daily household chores that needed to be done and allow Janelle some downtime.

If you feel your spouse can't seem to get back on their feet and may be experiencing depression or other mental health concerns, offer to help them talk to a counselor. Sometimes a person can't see in themselves what others are able to see.

If you are a coworker, follow the grieving mother's lead when she returns to work.

When your coworker arrives back on the job after her loss, it is important to give her space—but acknowledge your sympathies at the same time. Please don't stay silent or fail to acknowledge the loss.

Depending upon your relationship with your coworker, here are some ideas for how to address and sympathize with her:

- If you have a close relationship, visit your colleague in person shortly after her loss.
- Send a sympathy card in the mail. Write some words of encouragement or offer to take care of tasks. Say something helpful and encouraging, such as "Take your time to heal, we have it covered here at work."
- Address her loss when she returns. "I'm so sorry for your loss. Is there anything I can help you with today to make your transition back into work a little bit easier for you?"

If any of this is uncomfortable for you, a simple gesture can be all that is needed. Bring in a coffee or favorite beverage for your coworker and write a little note on the cup. Grab a flower and set it on their desk. Janelle had several colleagues who would pop their heads into the classroom and simply said, "I'm here for ten minutes, take a break" and "I've got this time with your students covered." Sometimes all it takes is for the grieving mother to know they are thought about.

Sometimes the bereaved mother doesn't know what she needs, and saying, "Let me know what you need" puts her in a difficult position. She may not be able to name her needs or want to ask for help, so being specific in what task you are offering to cover for her can be very helpful.

If you are a parent of a grieving mother, help with the other children in the household.

Watching your grown child suffer with intense pain is beyond hard. You don't know how to help and they don't know how to cope. Start by offering to take their other kids to school in the mornings or to dance class or ball practice in the evenings.

Be helpful with cleaning their house, running errands for her, and so on. Help out by allowing your daughter some alone, quiet time—but don't let this go on for too long. There is a fine line between enabling depression and being helpful. Take over some of the tasks and then gradually give them back to encourage the mother to get back on her feet.

You may not know what to do for a child (who is now an adult) suffering such loss. There may be generational differences that make it hard for you to understand what they are going through. There may be personal differences that separate the two of you and your ability to connect easily. Whatever those obstacles are, meet your child where they are. And keep offering to help.

If you are a sibling, reach out.

Family is a built-in community. It may not be comfortable for you, but if you find yourself in the role of a sibling to someone who's lost a baby, be there. Show up or call. Message your sibling. They may be sad or angry or even depressed.

It may seem like your sibling can't open up about their grief, but believe us when we say they want to. They will. So please be patient with them as they go through the roller coaster of joy and grief. It can take months for them to share. Put yourself aside and bear with them. Offer grace and a listening ear. Even if you can't or don't understand it, be thankful you don't, and try to recognize that this is life-altering for your sibling and they are navigating new territory.

Ask how your sibling is doing physically. Offer to cook dinner one evening, or if you don't live nearby, send a gift card for dinner or order them DoorDash. If your sibling has other children, offer to keep those nieces and nephews for a sleepover or an extended weekend.

If you are a neighbor, reach out.

Bring over a plate of cookies or a meal. Depending on the season of the year, drop off a vase of flowers on the porch or shovel the snow off their sidewalk. Most acts of helpfulness will be received and appreciated.

It's easy to feel like you are imposing or overstepping, but truth be told, when people are hurting, they may not know how to ask for help. Kelvi recalled getting a personalized note and an encouraging poem from a neighbor who had also experienced a miscarriage. "It was a sweet gesture to let me know I was not alone and she empathized with me." Janelle had a kind neighbor hand her a blue-and-pink ribbon pin to wear in honor of infant loss. Many neighbors brought food, handmade baby blankets, and beautiful jewelry. By knocking on the door, you are planting seeds of hope for each grieving mom.

If you are a friend, reach out.

Grieving people don't always seek others out. Honestly, many of them are just trying to survive. Even if you haven't spoken in years, we encourage you to take the time to call. If calling is too difficult, send a text. It doesn't have to be long—just let your friend know you are thinking about them. Let them know that God's got this. Message them a sweet quote or a daily photo of the sunrise. Just small gestures that open communication lines.

If you are a church family member, reach out and ask to put the mother and baby on your prayer list.

Ask the family experiencing loss if you may add them to your church's prayer list and send out communications to your church family for special prayers. Put both the baby and mother on your personal prayer list for a few weeks following the loss, and offer daily prayer intentions for mother and baby at your church service if you can.

Laurel's treasured white silk roses gifted by a friend in memory of her first two infant losses

You can even offer to take the family a meal or provide a gift card to a restaurant. Making small gestures make all the differences.

It gave Laurel some peace and comfort to know others had offered Mass intentions for her sweet Forrest. It let her know others were thinking about and praying for her family during their time of loss. Another friend who had also experienced loss from multiple miscarriages attended a special Mass offered for infant loss and brought Laurel two white silk roses with prayer cards for the infants she had lost up to that time. These roses have sat in a vase next to Laurel's bed since the day she brought them home in remembrance of her babies in Heaven.

If you are another mother who experienced loss, reach out and offer to share your story.

There is so much reassurance in being vulnerable and sharing your journey with others. For many, this kind of loss hasn't always been openly acknowledged, and it may not have felt acceptable to talk about—but from everything we are learning on our journeys, women *need* to talk about their babies. And we need all generations to speak up.

If you've never shared your story before, that's okay. Just make it clear that you also had a loss and you are opening yourself up now.

If you are willing to, ask the grieving mother if it's okay to share your story and see if they are willing to share theirs. They may not want to yet, and that is okay. Just letting them know they aren't alone can go a long way. Building that community of support helps enable you to take your grief and turn it into joy.

SURVIVING A MISCARRIAGE OR STILLBIRTH is hard even with a good support system. Without one, it can be lonely and devastating. Surviving miscarriage and child loss is undoubtedly hard for the mother, but it is also hard for others who grieve that baby. You may be a father, grandparent, aunt, uncle, close friend, or sibling of the baby who died. Perhaps you are a coworker, friend, or acquaintance of one of the surviving parents. You, too, do not have to stay silent. Reach out to others and tell them about your pain from the loss.

RECAP

Surviving Your Role as a Support System

Whether you are a family member, friend, or colleague, this section is designed to offer tips on how to support a grieving loved one.

- Don't minimize the loss.

- Don't stay silent.

- If you are a spouse, be patient with your partner.

- If you are a coworker, follow the grieving mother's lead when she returns to work.

- If you are a parent of a grieving mother, help with the other children in the household.

- If you are a sibling, reach out.

- If you are a neighbor, reach out.

- If you are a friend, reach out.

- If you are a church family member, reach out and ask to put the mother and baby on your prayer list.

- If you are another mother who experienced loss, reach out and offer to share your story.

Journeying with Joy and Grief

 *Peace is that calmness that is only from Christ and is in my heart, my actions, and thoughts regardless of the day and the situation.*

—Janelle's journal entry

 *I am so grateful even if my heart feels frozen and I emotionlessly flip through pictures of Facebook posts. It does touch my heart. This is the day the Lord has made.*

—Janelle's journal entry

The distance between joy and sorrow is measured by a heartbeat.

—Author unknown

THERE ARE SOME AMAZING MOMENTS in life that are just pure joy. They are bliss. Moments that make your whole being beam with pride and excitement. Moments that etch themselves in your life. They leave a lasting imprint on your soul because they are wholesome and thrilling and pure.

There are moments like that in each of our lives. Sometimes we have to dig deep to find them, but they are there. These are moments that you want to treasure forever. Holding your own newborn children can be moments like this. Moments when you are just bursting with excitement and enjoyment.

When you can feel that deep love down to your core. Maybe it was walking down the aisle on your wedding day. Or watching your niece or nephew graduate high school. Whatever that moment is for you, it's euphoric. And because you know that feeling exists, you desire more of it. It fills you with so much hope. It can almost feel overwhelming. We know that feeling. It's a beautiful feeling, and you are allowed to feel it.

And then there are also times when your heart feels heavy and your body is emotionally weighed down. There are times when you can't imagine being happy, when you can't even muster a smile. It may be at the loss of a loved one or a devastating career change. Whatever the exact situation, your body feels that weight. It seeps into your bones and you ache. You long. That deep feeling of grief and sadness can wash over you and interrupt your days and even your weeks. Grief and sadness can etch themselves into your life. So how can you have the feelings of deep grief and heartbreak, devastation and soul-crushing pain, at the same time as joy? How is it that losing a child, a precious tiny being, can be both these feelings?

In our disbelief and confusion of emotions, we think these two feelings are contrasting. That they can't happen simultaneously. But in our experiences, grief and joy coincide. They are rooted in the same level of our human experiences. They are both deep and compounding. They are not surface emotions or simple feelings. They are complex emotions that stir your inner being. They set your soul on fire. They stir something in you that everyday experiences don't, and because they are such deep emotions from complex situations, they can happen concurrently. As Annie Anderson—author of *Your Soul Is Wintering*—noted in her blog post dated March 24, 2022, "Grief only exists and has a place in our lives because love did first." You love big, so you grieve big.

In January 2019, only seven weeks after Laurel's loss, she received the wonderful news that her sister had her baby—a beautiful baby boy! When she found out she had a new nephew, Jameson, she was so happy to know he and her sister were safe and the sweet, new baby was healthy. Laurel was also overcome by grief and ugly-cried herself to sleep that night—she just sobbed. With the arrival of her nephew, she should be preparing to meet their precious baby in one month as Forrest's due date was coming up. Her husband, Bryce, told her the same thing the next morning: He was so overjoyed for his in-laws and the beautiful addition to their family, but he was so sad they wouldn't be bringing their own baby boy home to their family. Bryce and Laurel were both also happy to learn Laurel's sister had a boy (they hadn't found out the gender during their pregnancy) but so sad because these two boy cousins would never get to meet on Earth and play together—they would have been awesome buddies. So much happiness and so much sadness at the same time.

You can't let grief control you.

The complexities of love and the nonlinear path of grief are big situations to process. They are huge emotions, and they can change your body's chemical makeup. Now, we are no physicians or medical experts, but we are aware of the body-altering effects emotions have on humans. Feelings change us. All experiences and the emotions that go with them change us. So why would we expect two seemingly different emotions not to change us or happen in tandem? You can't experience grief or joy in the exact same way as anyone else. It is personal and soul-specific.

But just like all feelings, even something as heart-wrenching as loss, you can't let grief control you. We'll say it again: You can't let grief control you. Grief has its place. Grief is affirming. Grief is valid. Grief needs your time and attention. But grief can't take up *all* your time. You need to express that deep grief. It needs its turn in your life, your day, and your healing. And every time you let it surface and be expressed in a healthy way, you honor it—and honor the joy that is found in grief.

Don't hesitate to share your pain. If the pain feels like it's bubbling up inside of you, then acknowledge it in one of the ways you find helpful and healthy. Let it have its moment in your day and in your path. But then, just like you would with any emotion, move from it. Some days it'll be easier to let grief in and then shut it back down. Some days are more convenient than others for grief to play a role. But don't let those be excuses for not working on yourself and healing yourself from your soul out. "Ten years later, and I think I can finally say I'm ready to work on healing my outside. I'm ready to take the step of healing what grief has done to my physical body," said Janelle.

Healing takes time. Grief takes effort. Joy takes the impossible and makes it bearable.

When we women talk about our journey—when we share our hearts and our survival stories—it's intended to open a conversation, to offer a perspective of joy in grief. It's to be a knock on your door to say, "I'm so sorry you are going through this," "I see you," and "you are not alone." So no matter where, what, or how you are managing, know that our words are expressed in love for you and all your babies.

And your story matters.

The generations before ours often never spoke of their miscarriages or stillbirths. The heartache and tears that these women shared with us 30+ years later told us that not only did they love those babies, but they never forgot about them and still hold them close every day. The love you have for your child will never leave, but the heaviness of the loss will eventually lift. No matter if it has been two days, two weeks, two years, or two decades, you don't have to suffer in silence—and you can survive it. We must be loud enough in the silence that those who have been silent and those who feel pressured to keep silent have a voice. That more stories will be shared and more healing can happen. We must find a voice so that the women who come after us don't feel that pressure. That they will find ways to walk the path of loss a little more lightly.

RECAP

Journeying with Joy and Grief

There is no finish line for grief, but you can learn to heal. Allow yourself to feel joy during your tough days.

- Joy and grief can coexist.

- It is okay to feel both at the same time.

- Grief is not a place to stay.

- Healing takes time, but joy makes it possible.

Stopping the Silence

There is no greater agony than bearing an untold story inside you.

—Maya Angelou

Through memory, love transcends the limits of time and offers hope at any moment of our lives.

—Henri Nouwen

ONE OF THE BIGGEST TAKEAWAYS we want you to gain from this collection of memories and survival tools is that you can be the stopgap for the next generation when talking about miscarriage, infant loss, and mental health. You can be the person who puts an end to the silence surrounding miscarriage and the mental struggles that follow. Your story, your experiences, will be a vehicle for you to help change the way the next generation encounters grief.

You can be the stopgap for the next generation when talking about miscarriage, infant loss, and mental health.

We have each interacted with women who have suffered loss and who struggle to share that hurt and sadness with others. Women who have carried the hurt for decades and have buried it deep down inside, tucked away until it is almost inaccessible. But these women still carry the heaviness of that loss, each and every day. We need to step up for these women and share what we know. We need to speak up for the generations to come. We need to not only be a stopgap generation but offer something more lasting. Tools. Survival tips. An outlet. We need to take this uncomfortable air around loss and fix it. We need women to stop the silent suffering no matter the length of term. We need to think about how we can be a part of the survival tips for each generation. Because each generation needs us and our stories.

Kelvi recalled, "I slid into the pew the first Sunday back in church after my loss. I purposefully selected a seat by the window for an easy escape if need be; plus, most people walked down the center aisle, so I wouldn't have to greet or acknowledge folks walking in. I was hoping no one would approach me or say anything to me as I was doing everything I could just to hold myself together.

"My hope was cut short after just a few minutes. An older woman with the most beautiful silver hair came up to me and just squeezed my hand. The tears in her eyes told me that her empathy was genuine. 'I'm so sorry for your loss,' she said. 'It will take some time, but it does get better.' *Wow,* I thought to myself. *I had no idea she lost a baby.* I never knew, and no one ever said.

"A few minutes later, another one of my church sisters came and sat in the pew right in front of me. She turned around, grabbed my hand, and tried to hold back her own tears as she said, 'One of these days I'm going to come over and we are going to have a really long talk, but not yet,' she told me. Her voice cracked, and it was at that time I realized she too had experienced a loss. She was in her early 60s, and I thought, *Whoa—she can barely talk about her loss, and it has to be at least 20–30 years later.* I was never told of her loss either, but I later learned that both of these sweet ladies had babies buried out in the church cemetery adjacent to our sanctuary. *I wonder what their names are,* I thought to myself. *I wonder why these women never talk about their loss. I wonder if they still suffer in silence.*"

It is heartbreaking that women can't and don't share their losses. We can be the source of encouragement for others, and we can make a difference for future women. Healing is available to those who seek it. Healing is a choice of the mind, if not of the heart. And if we give our emotions permission to appear and open our hearts to sharing our journey of loss and hurt and mental health needs, we don't have to suffer in silence.

Perhaps it's not the silence of women who've walked this journey before us. Perhaps it's the silence of the women and young girls to come. If you have children of your own already, what a testimony that can be to them to say, "Hey, Mom is not okay right now. But you know what, she is taking the right steps to get there and getting the help she needs." We need to stop hiding our ugly feelings from those around us, especially our kids. They need to learn that not everything is going to be okay in life. Not everything in life is easy, and they need to know how to correctly manage those feelings when life takes them down those nasty roads of loss, heartache, bullying, and disappointment.

Sharing our journey paves a path for the women after us who will suffer loss. By being open and honest about our hurt and our health, we are giving future women a more solid foundation to survive on. There is nothing weak about seeking help. There is nothing to be ashamed of when sharing your feelings. If you are bold enough to seek help, then you deserve help. You deserve support and encouragement. You are opening a door for the next generation to see how survival can happen. We can do better for each other by supporting individuals who are seeking help. We shouldn't tear them down or shame them for getting help. We believe the majority of those people who learn that you are going to counseling will praise you. They may even secretly envy you. The truth is, you have taken a step of bravery. It takes courage to make that first call or send that first email to a counselor.

What a shame it would be to keep the survival skills we've learned to ourselves. To never share with others how we made it to our next tomorrow.

You have the opportunity to take your pain and turn it into a purpose. To change the path for yourself and for generations to come by speaking when you could be silent. By sharing when you could hide in shame. To shift the focus from what has happened to us to what we can now do for those who come after us. What an amazing gift we can give to others by saying, "Me too," "I understand," and "I survived." What a shame it would be to keep the survival skills we've learned to ourselves. To never share with others how we made it to our next tomorrow. It would be a disappointment to not bless these future women with the knowledge we have gained first-hand from our journeys of turning grief into joy. We encourage you to take the opportunity to be part of stopping the silence.

Stopping the silence requires us to be bold. It requires us to find brave friends. To *be* brave friends. It means we show up on the doorstep of the next woman who finds herself on this path of living without her baby. We show up to support, uplift, and encourage. Stopping the silence means taking the journey you've been called to one step at a time. A journey in joy and grief. A journey that we three women believe you can survive.

Surviving your loss is the greatest story you can tell. And that story will help us all stop the silence.

RECAP

Stopping the Silence

Generations of women have suffered in silence surrounding miscarriage and infant loss. We are here to tell you that you no longer have to. You CAN talk about it, and by doing so, you help not only yourself but the next generation to come.

- Seeking the help you need is bravery.
- Be vulnerable enough to tell your story.

- Be the stopgap for the next generation.
- Be encouraging to others and show up for them.

Afterword

Living with grief is a beautiful tribute. A tribute to yourself, to your child, and to God. It exhibits a peace beyond understanding, a love greater than the here and now. Living is the next thing you can do for your child. Breathing in the hardness of grief while also inhaling the goodness of God's grace into you. Those breaths are the very existence of strength. They are the ultimate survival gift you can give to yourself and your story. Your very breath is a tribute you can give not only to your story of loss and love but to others who need to hear from you.

There is a world full of women who need to hear your story. They need to be encouraged by your strength. They want to be encouraged by you. And by honoring that great love for your baby and speaking out is exactly the gift you can give to others. Living. Breathing. Inhaling and exhaling. Kelvi, Janelle, and Laurel breathe that goodness each minute of every day. They spend their days completing the daily call of following God, waking each day to try and honor His call in their lives and trying to bring joy to others. Part of their tribute is building a support system for each other and for other women.

KELVI MOTHERS THREE beautiful and very active girls. She lives on the same beloved, bustling street and hosts "Crafts with Kelvi" for the kids on the block to get her creative energy out after selling the flower shop a year after losing Karaline—all the time being in love with her husband of 17 years, Karlton.

Kelvi shared, "My biggest takeaway from this book journey has been how liberating it is to work through all of the emotions of miscarriage. The pain and sadness no longer dictate other areas of my life, and the fragility of my emotions is gone. I reflect on how I couldn't even say the name Karaline, and now I'm able to talk about my loss to other women as a way to offer guidance and support."

LAUREL WALKS INTO her mixed-animal veterinary clinic each day to meet with her clients and their animals and offer her support and knowledge. Each evening, she comes home to raise her three beautiful biological children and two wonderful bonus children with her caring husband, Bryce. Laurel thoroughly enjoys motherhood and tries to soak up all the little things, trying to see the beauty and simplicity of life through the eyes of three children under the age of four.

"Writing a book is something I absolutely never thought I would do," Laurel reflected. "What an utterly daunting task for me! I am not a writer —I am a 'doer,' and I always just want to help people. My hope for writing this book is that if we can help at least one person get through their loss and heartache and give them even a little glimmer of hope, then this whole process was worth it for me. What I didn't expect to get out of this book-writing experience was an even greater sense of healing on my never-ending journey of change. I've been so blessed to be able to form these beautiful friendships and also work on my journey of faith. God is so good."

AS THIS BOOK is being published, Janelle marks her tenth year without Eli on Earth. She finished 19 years of teaching and 14 years of coaching to embrace a new chapter of life. She continues to raise four fantastic children in the small town in which she grew up with her husband, Kirk, a stone artist and volunteer firefighter. Janelle thrives on following her kids in their schooling and their many activities.

"This process of remembering and revisiting my personal losses as a mother has, in a unique way, brought about a reconnection to things I have put away, a reconnecting to what I have been through. It has brought an opportunity to find some missing pieces and rebuild some of my inner strength. Strength in my way of handling adversity. Strength in my belief in others. Strength in God's calling for my life. I have been called to live a purposeful life. A life that can balance both the pain of the past and the joy of things to come. I can have a life that honors what was lost and also live for what is to come. A life that doesn't fear pain, but one that uses pain for growth. By reconnecting to some lost and hidden pieces of my life, I feel a sense of peace. A sense of reconciliation. This process has brought into my life bold, sit-at-my-table forever friends. It has brought a new layer of healing to my loss. This process has brought reconciliation with my new self where I can allow myself to journey into the tomorrows without hating all of my pasts. Reconciliation. Reconnections. And remembrance. The path that this process has put me on fills me with all of that and the promises of more. This is another path in my journey."

EACH OF US WOMEN—Laurel, Kelvi, and Janelle—has a new understanding of loss and love. Of joy and grief. We carry these life messages with us each day, lessons that continue to shape us even while creating this book. Spending their last twelve months of collaborating, putting together thoughts, reviewing past journals, and writing down steps toward the possibility of helping more people created a rhythm of joy and grief that drove them toward writing *Surviving the Silence*—a book that brings words to the silent pain of child loss and—hopefully—healing to its readers.

With this book, we step into the next chapters of our lives with you. We want nothing more than to help you survive the silence.

Your Story

_____

_____

_____

_____

_____

_____

_____

_____

_____

_____

_____

_____

_____

_____

_____

_____

_____

_____

_____

_____

_____

BLESSINGS THAT CAN BRING JOY DURING GRIEF

- *Rain on a summer day*
- *A fresh breeze in the window*
- *Bare feet on a tiled floor*
- *A game of catch in the living room*
- *The jingle of dog tags*
- *A choir rehearsing*
- *Buttery popcorn*
- *A moment of silence*
- *The colors of the sunrise*
- *The blow of indoor air conditioning*
- *Dew on a spider's web*
- *A friendly message*
- *Safe drivers*
- *The clink of ice in a glass*
- *Clouds of all sizes*
- *Fall leaves*
- *Laughter during a car ride*
- *A pot of chili*
- *A fiancé's smile*
- *Fuzzy socks on a cold day*
- *Playdough creations*

Resources

Anderson, Annie. "Timelines." *Your Soul Is Wintering* (blog). Published March 24, 2022. https://www.annieanderson.co.nz/blog/timelines/.

Nynas, Julie, Priya Narang, Manjeet K. Kolikonda, and Steven Lippmann. "Depression and Anxiety Following Early Pregnancy Loss: Recommendations for Primary Care Providers." *The Primary Care Companion for CNS Disorders* 17, no. 1 (2015). https://doi.org/10.4088/PCC.14r01721.

About the Authors

Dr. Laurel Davis, Kelvi Place, and Janelle Robson live in central Kansas with their families. Together, they are helping to break the silence around pregnancy loss and providing words of encouragement and tools grieving parents have long been needing.

www.ingramcontent.com/pod-product-compliance
Lightning Source LLC
Chambersburg PA
CBHW021151130626
46554CB00005B/1767